This book is a grace-filled gift. In blended families, possessiveness divides while grace connects. Reading *Grace-Filled Stepparenting* feels like sitting with a wise friend who is gently leading you through the unknown into connection. Laurie Polich Short will help you find grace for your home.

—**Ron Deal**, bestselling author of *The Smart Stepfamily*, coauthor of *Building Love Together in Blended Families*, and director of FamilyLife Blended®

This book is filled with hope and practical wisdom by a woman who has lived out these principles in her own journey. I've known Laurie most of her adult life, and I find her, like this book, refreshingly authentic. She is a wonderful communicator and a great storyteller with truth and lots of grace.

—**Jim Burns**, president, HomeWord, author of *The Purity Code* and *Doing Life with Your Adult Children: Keep Your Mouth Shut and the Welcome Mat Out*

Laurie has been an insightful writer on difficult topics. There is none more difficult than stepparenting, and this grace-filled book will help anyone turn what can be a nightmare into a great blessing.

—**Steve Arterburn**, bestselling author, host of *New Life Live!*, and founder of the Women of Faith conferences

With 40 percent of all families being stepfamilies, this book brings needed hope! It's not only an amazing resource for stepparents—every church and minister should have it in their library as the go-to resource for this growing community of struggling and searching-for-help parents. I've known and worked with Laurie for many years, and her experience and wisdom as a stepmom make this book a must-read for anyone trying to navigate this challenging road with grace.

—**Doug Fields**, author, youth pastor, and founder of Downloadyouthministry.com

Laurie Short has written a book filled with practical help and hope for stepparents. Every stepmom and stepdad will find a wealth of encouragement in these pages. *Grace-Filled Stepparenting* shows you how to keep loving your kids—no matter how long it takes or how thick the emotional walls may seem.

—**Les & Leslie Parrott**, #1 *New York Times* bestselling
authors of *Saving Your Marriage Before It Starts*

Laurie Polich Short has done an excellent job of weaving her stepfamily's story into a resource that contains deep biblical wisdom and compassion. With a humble heart, Laurie explores how acts of kindness and daily tenacity—even in complex and challenging situations—can lead to victory.

—**Laura Petherbridge**, international speaker, stepmom,
and author of *The Smart Stepmom* (with Ron Deal)
and *When I Do Becomes I Don't*

Grace-Filled Step Parenting

Grace-Filled Step Parenting

Laurie Polich Short

HARVEST HOUSE PUBLISHERS
EUGENE, OREGON

Grace-Filled Stepparenting
Copyright © 2021 by Laurie Polich Short
Published by Harvest House Publishers
Eugene, Oregon 97408
www.harvesthousepublishers.com

ISBN 978-0-7369-8235-1 (pbk.)
ISBN 978-0-7369-8236-8 (eBook)

Library of Congress Cataloging-in-Publication Data

Names: Polich-Short, Laurie, author.
Title: Grace-filled stepparenting / Laurie Polich Short.
Description: Eugene, Oregon : Harvest House Publishers, [2021] | Includes
   bibliographical references.
Identifiers: LCCN 2020054242 (print) | LCCN 2020054243 (ebook) | ISBN
   9780736982351 (paperback) | ISBN 9780736982368 (ebook)
Subjects: LCSH: Parenting—Religious aspects—Christianity. |
   Stepfamilies—Religious aspects—Christianity. | Stepparents—Religious
   life. | Stepparents—Anecdotes.
Classification: LCC BV4529 .P645 2021 (print) | LCC BV4529 (ebook) | DDC
   248.8/45—dc23
LC record available at https://lccn.loc.gov/2020054242
LC ebook record available at https://lccn.loc.gov/2020054243

For Jordan

Since the day your dad and I married,
you have owned a piece of my heart.
You always will.

Acknowledgments

Special thanks to…

The steps, halves, and nonrelated loved ones who make up my pieced-together family.

Vivian, Linda, and Natalie, who make motherhood and daughterhood very loose terms.

My dad's beloved wife, Bernie, whose grace filters our Polich story.

My editor, Gene, who gently and expertly held my manuscript after I squirmed and cried my way through.

And finally, my amazing husband, Jere, for without him this book would not exist.

Contents

Introduction

My stepson gave me permission to write this book.

Writers inadvertently bring their loved ones into the limelight, so it would seem disingenuous to write a book about stepparenting without asking your stepchild how he felt about it first. I told him I could try changing his name, but there would be some obvious problems given the fact that I write nonfiction and we live in the same house.

I always knew in my heart I wanted to write this book, but timing was an issue, and the end of my stepson's high school years seemed the right time to do it. The more years I've been able to actually live as a stepmom, the more I've been given to say. But first I had to make sure he was okay with me saying it.

Our hope is that this book will help you navigate this tender dance between you and your stepchild whatever your particular situation has given you. Your circumstances are probably different from mine, but some of the challenges and joys are likely the same. I pray this book will touch your story in the places where you need to know you are seen, and that it may extend to you some wisdom, encouragement, and hope.

My stepson turned seventeen this year, so I knew he would say no if he didn't want our story to be told. I am grateful to him for saying yes, for he not only gave me the gift of being able to reflect on one of the most important relationships of my life, he also graciously extended that gift to you.

As of 2017, 40 percent of all married couples with children are forming so-called blended families, and the number of stepparents continues to increase each year. I presume because you picked up this book you either are one, have one, know one, or are thinking about becoming one. Being a stepparent is hard, and there is no "one size fits all" stepparenting manual to follow. Relationships in blended families are not always happy, they are never easy, and some people in them wish they weren't there at all. However, if you go into stepparenting with an open heart to whatever your situation has for you, it will deepen your capacity to love and teach you grace in a way no other role can.

Stepparenting is a calling, and like any other mission field, you have no idea what will ultimately happen. You only know that in marrying a parent, you married someone whose family story began before you entered the picture. This decision will stretch you for the rest of your life, but it doesn't have to break you. In fact, if you hold on in tough times, it may make you stronger and more fulfilled than you ever thought you could be. It's probably not the story you imagined when you thought about having a family. But if you are called to marry someone with children, it's the story God has given you to live.

May this book cheer you on in your journey.

1

Welcome to the Pool

Becoming a stepparent is like standing on the edge of a pool, wondering how far you should go in. There are people in the pool, and one of them—your new spouse—is beckoning you in with open arms. Others have their back toward you, hoping you'll take as little as possible of their space. In the middle of the pool are the ones everyone came to swim with, and if they are younger than eight, they are probably waving at you. If they are five or six, they might even be calling your name. If they are teenagers or adults, they may be pretending you are not there. Worse yet, they could be wishing it.

Should you play it safe and dip your feet in the shallow end? Or should you take your chances and dive in?

You probably can't avoid getting at least partially wet, and more so if a child ends up living with you. But how deep you go into the pool is determined by how much risk your heart is willing to take. That choice will likely be determined by how fragile your heart is, how supported you feel by others, and whether you are counting on something in return for what you give. Amelia Watkins writes that "stepparenting is a daunting task, because it requires transitioning from stranger to parental figure in the eyes of someone who has a previously established parentage."[1]

In other words, the pool is already full when you are invited in.

I negotiated my feelings about stepparenting long before I became one myself because my parents are divorced and remarried. Having stepparents slightly altered my perspective on being one, giving me a little more grace and understanding in my role. But ultimately, I learned what every stepparent learns: The depth of gratitude and love and pain and discomfort you feel is directly tied to how much of your heart you decide to give. And if you weigh the cost and decide to give your whole heart, I can tell you by experience that you will be changed.

So, this is my story of coming to the pool. And making the decision to jump in.

BEGINNINGS

Growing up, I had dreams of becoming a mom, but those dreams always assumed biology. I never imagined that I would marry at forty-nine or that when a child came into my life, he would be six. I don't believe anyone hopes to become a stepparent, nor do boys and girls grow up dreaming they'll be a second spouse. Those dreams come out of unexpected turns and brokenness. Brokenness is generally overlooked when we plot out our life.

As a youth pastor, I mentored many kids who called me Mom, and when I got engaged in my early forties, I had a biological shot at becoming one. That opportunity disappeared when my engagement broke up, and that story is in another book. Grace crashed in with a second chance at marriage, and this time I made it down the aisle. As a bonus, there were two men waiting for me at the altar—one was six feet two, breathtakingly handsome, and my age. The other was three feet nine with curly blond hair. He was holding the pillow with the ring. My husband's six-year-old son was the gift that came with my marriage, and even though he came packaged with another mom, I was starry-eyed at God's generosity. Loss raises the volume of grace, even when it comes with a caveat. What I didn't know was how God would use that caveat to stretch me more than anything before or since.

All marriages begin with love and hope, even if there are complexities peering at you from behind your bouquet. Those complexities were seated in the first two rows at my wedding, where my divorced parents sat across the aisle from each other with their spouses, along with half-sisters and stepsiblings, who were all a part of my family since my parents' remarriages. Statistics reveal that at least 40 percent of all US families are stepfamilies,[2] although the dynamics of each family can vary with the ages of the children and circumstances of the adults. They can grow to be flourishing or disastrous, depending on the circumstances and relationships that evolve from the mix. I hope this book encourages you that there is a long story unfolding when it comes to stepparenting. Your persevering love will make a difference in the way your stepfamily evolves. It may never be a traditional family, but it can still be a beautiful one, for God is a master at putting broken pieces together into a new whole.

As an adult stepchild, I understood a little of the journey I was embarking on, though I had experienced it from a slightly different angle than my stepson. My blended story was different because it came much later in life, but the challenge of accommodating more than two parents is an experience we both share. My father remarried when I turned twenty-two, and on the day he asked a twenty-five-year-old to share his name, the pain of stretching my name to include her was wrapped in thin veneer. I still look at pictures of their wedding and feel sad, though time has unveiled the strength of my stepmother's heart. "She's a keeper," I whisper to the girl in the photos who was once me, "and one day you will know it."

Since that day, my stepmom has stood by my father through cancer, recovery, and aging, and she has remained devoted to him for thirty-six years. However, the day they married, I thought my heart would implode, and this proves your stepfamily journey can evolve and change. I am increasingly grateful for my stepmother, even with our three-year age difference, so let that be an encouragement for any stepparent to cling to during difficult times. My stepmom has even become an example to me in my own stepparenting, which affirms that you never know all that God will do with the brokenness in your life. Fix your eyes on the long view.

When I was thirty-six, my mom married a retired minister who was eleven years older than her. He had four grown children and two grandkids when he entered the marriage, so he settled for any level of friendship my brothers and I would give him. In my survey of more than a hundred stepparents, those who entered marriage when the children were adults reported that their relationships varied from acquaintances to wonderful friendships. The dynamics of older stepfamilies aren't quite as complicated as younger stepfamilies because everyone has more freedom to go at their own pace. Second marriages that occur later in life may complicate holidays or create competition between grandparents, but these disruptions are minimal compared to a young stepfamily's blended life.

If given a choice, most children would choose to have their biological parents together, but it *is* possible for a good second marriage to enrich a child's life. This depends partly on the relationship that evolves between the stepparent and stepchild, but there are many examples of successful stepfamilies that offer this hope. When I entered my marriage, my husband and I wanted to be able to give an example of a good marriage to the boy we committed to parent. But we also knew we were embarking on a daunting journey, because the road to forming a stepfamily is unescapably full of curves and bumps.

You don't have to poke too far into the internet to uncover the stress and anxiety that can accompany stepparenting. The stress seems to especially impact stepmoms, who are twice as likely as biological moms to be depressed.[3] (At the time of this writing, the most-reviewed step-parenting book is titled *Stepmonster*, which not so subtly proclaims the stigma many of us face. Though the book has some very helpful information, I hid the cover when someone exercised next to me at the gym.)

Nothing can prepare you for every trial you will face as a step-parent, but there are some insights that can help equip you for the challenges ahead. You will be called to love bravely in an often thankless role. My hope is that this book will encourage you that the journey is worth it because God will use stepparenting to grow your soul. C.S. Lewis declared that "to love at all is to be vulnerable; love anything and your heart will be wrung and possibly broken."[4] While this is true in all relationships, it may be especially true for stepparents, because you learn to love with no strings attached. You will always be a child's choice.

Stepparenting isn't for the faint of heart because it requires sacrifice and courage. You can minimize your role by keeping your heart closed, but you will miss out on the gift that will enlarge your soul. By parenting a child who isn't yours, you have the opportunity to love unconditionally, which is the part of you God longs to grow. Love is best and brightest when it is delivered with open hands, and stepparenting will present you with that chance. You will learn in your job description what all parents discover when their children leave home: Our children don't belong to us. They are given to us to nurture and build into, and as a stepparent, you will be a part of that process in your child's life. You may only be an add-on parent, but if you embrace your role and live it for all its worth, you will have a unique voice in their growth. You may not share biology or be listed on their birth certificate, but you can heal broken places and bring an objectivity that biological parents don't always have. The joy will be yours to quietly celebrate as you watch your stepchild flourish, because you will know the commitment you made to your parenting played a part.

Now that Jordan is seventeen, I thought it was a good time to add my voice to the books on stepparenting and provide some hope for those who share this call. I wanted to wait until I had a decade of experience under my belt, and for Jordan to be old enough to contribute his insights. I believe his perspective will add value (however risky that might be for me), and I also have the input of more than a hundred stepparents I surveyed to supplement our story. Some challenges are common to every stepparent, but I pray that the words you need will grow bold on the page and encourage your soul.

If you are reading this book before you become a stepparent, I commend you for thinking ahead to prepare for this role. Just the fact that you picked up this book and are reading it before your marriage means you recognize the seriousness of the task. When you are pursuing a relationship with someone who has a child, it involves more than figuring out whether that person is right for you. You will be marrying the children who come with your spouse, so you must decide whether being a stepparent is something you are ready to embrace. After you cross the altar, you will be a parent, so take time to see all that is before you as you take each step. There are other hearts involved in the decisions you make.

Your relationship with your spouse's child officially begins the day you get married; but you start to build the foundation for that relationship as soon as you get serious with someone who has kids. For that reason, every move you make in your relationship with that child needs to be made with intention—but you also have to make room for every unexpected surprise. It's good practice for what life as a stepparent will bring.

THE STORY OF MEETING MY MEN

Jere and I had been seeing each other only three months when it happened. My future stepson "outed" me at my church. This wasn't a church I attended; it was a church where I was an associate pastor, and as a forty-eight-year-old single woman, I tried to keep my dating life under wraps. I had decided to keep this one area private because so much of my life was under scrutiny. I was also frequently approached with, "There's someone I want you to meet." However, on this particular day, my relationship with Jere went public before we intended for people to know. It was the first of many wonderful interruptions Jere's little boy would bring to my life.

Before meeting Jere, my dating had been less than thrilling; it had basically boiled down to whose baggage could be compatible with mine. After another mediocre relationship had fizzled, some friends invited me to a party so I could meet their newly single friend. Not wanting to block any opportunity, I reluctantly agreed. When I got to the party, our immediate chemistry caused my heart to take an unfamiliar leap. I believe my stomach did an actual somersault when he asked if we could meet for coffee the following week.

We met down the street from where he worked, and I tried to appear nonchalant while stomach butterflies clamored for my attention. During our conversation, he shared that he was a stepdad as well as a biological dad; he had raised two stepchildren for twelve years while he was married to his ex-wife. Since his ex-wife left, his third child was the only one who belonged to him. The stepchildren were now only connected to him by their choice. This was the first time I came face to face with the risk involved in stepparenting—it was evident that his heart was grieving this loss. I met Jere during a painful chapter with his stepkids, and it gave me a chance to deeply ponder what becoming a stepparent would mean. I had to ponder it because Jere's biological son was part of any future with him. Being a father was clearly the crux of his heart and life.

After three months of dating, we were pretty clear that our relationship was becoming serious, so we decided it was time for me to meet Jere's son. Opinions vary as to when this should happen, but you should eventually see what your relationship will be like with the child involved. Many couples "practice" stepparenting by living together first, but this is risky because of the bonding that can mess up a child's heart. Statistics reveal that the more transitions kids have to make with the adults who parent them, the more likely there will be problems in their development and growth.[5] Ultimately, our faith commitment precluded that option anyway; we had decided that marriage would be the only way we'd set up house. We went the traditional route from dating to marriage, and three months into our relationship, I began building a friendship with Jere's child.

I figured homemade cookies were a safe bet, and the minute I laid eyes on him, I was smitten. One parent on my survey said, "Don't become a stepparent unless you love your future stepchildren." The day I met Jordan, I was putty in his hands. After he gobbled down three of my cookies and hugged me, my heart was drawn even closer to Jere. After that day, Jordan referred to me as "the cookie lady," and this became my nickname the first few weeks I was in his life. This is when the incident occurred at church.

Because Jere and I were keeping our relationship private, we sat separately even though we attended the same service at our church. We were waiting to sit together until we were more established in our relationship so we'd be ready for the questions that would inevitably come. However, on this particular day, Jere's sweet golden-haired boy made a decision that took our plan out of our hands. As I took my seat in the front of the church, I heard Jordan yell out, "Dad, there's the cookie lady!" Before Jere could stop him, he yanked him down the aisle to where I sat in the second row. I froze. Jordan plopped down next to me and put his dad on the other side of him, and then he took my arm and put it around his shoulders. Then he carefully took his dad's arm and put it around his shoulders from the other side. Within minutes we were seated in front of my church with a little boy snuggled between us. Jere and I kept our eyes locked forward, but we felt the stares of hungry church ladies watching our backs.

Though it was briefly uncomfortable, I have to admit it was also wonderful because it was the first time I felt acceptance from my future

stepson. Somewhere in his five-year-old brain, he decided that day that he wanted me close to him and his dad. It meant the world to me, and I was willing to go public because of it. It wasn't the last time my carefully constructed plans would be interrupted by this boy. From that day forward, I learned that as a stepparent, I would sometimes be called to choose my stepchild's comfort over my own. If you become a stepparent, you will likely be faced with the same choice.

Studies reveal that if you are a high-control (perhaps firstborn?) stepparent, you will probably experience more challenges in your stepparenting.[6] I didn't realize I'd have my first practice letting go of my control before I even got engaged. That day in church I had two choices. I could remove Jordan's arm from my shoulders or live with the fact that there would be gossip hell to pay. I chose the second option, and it was the first of many times my love for my stepson would direct my response.

Maybe lack of control is a good place to start when you are asking yourself if you can handle being a stepparent. How much control are you willing to give up? Marriage itself requires sacrifice, but when you add stepchildren, the sacrifice is infinitely greater. It's best to think this through when dating a parent, before your feelings take you into a multilevel commitment you aren't prepared to make.

On top of all this, it isn't just your spouse's child who you will be marrying; your vows will include your spouse's ex, who comes with your child. Another stepparent may be added to the mix when your spouse's ex remarries. Picturing all the people you are marrying when you say "I do" to someone with kids is not very romantic, but it certainly is more accurate. Your "I do" extends not only past your spouse to their children, but also to the biological parent who shares (and exceeds) your place. The fantasy of happily ever after with you, your spouse, and your stepchild is just that—a fantasy. There may be seasons (or days) when you will be with your little family, but you have to be prepared for the many times it will be chopped up or shifted around. The health and well-being of your stepchildren are tied to their other biological parent, and you will need to constantly make space for their place. You can put out the welcome mat or have your door shoved in, but they are part of the package your marriage brought to your life. The best way to go into stepparenting is to get ready to open your heart (and door) to the adventure ahead.

NEW THINGS TAKE TIME

When you first begin forming your stepfamily, it's important to remember you are forming a new context for the love and growth that began in a family that no longer exists. Loss and brokenness set the stage for your family, so at times, you may feel as if you cannot see your way through the mess. God speaks to the prophet Isaiah about what He is going to do for people who are coming out of loss and brokenness, and two images in the passage are very appropriate for stepfamilies: "See, I am doing a new thing! Now it springs up; do you not perceive it? I am making *a way in the wilderness* and *streams in the wasteland*" (Isaiah 43:19).

A way in the wilderness. Streams in the wasteland. These might be two of the best descriptions you'll find for what you are trying to do in stepparenting. Some of the people coming into your stepfamily will feel like they have been (or are) in a wilderness or wasteland. But God can make a way to a new future if you commit to staying the course. Thinking of your stepfamily as a *way* or a *path* rather than a destination will help you remember the process takes time.

A way in the wilderness takes you through stark conditions. Streams in the wasteland have less than ideal surroundings while they provide life and hope. These descriptions can help you hold to your mission even when things look bleak. Your marriage will begin by helping a child (or children) settle into broken pieces of family, so you will contend with imperfect conditions even if you are headed the right way. You need to be prepared for more adversity than couples who start with a clean slate.

Some may feel it's a liability to begin this way, but it can also be a gift. You will learn how adept you are as a couple in making difficult adjustments, and how you handle responsibility and adversity when you are not always prepared. These challenges are inevitable in every marriage, but stepparenting gives you an opportunity to face them earlier. If you can weather the difficulties of forming a stepfamily, you will build a foundation with your spouse that is tested and strong.

No one can predict the adversities that will hit your stepfamily, but when you have a strong foundation of faith, you will be better equipped to survive your challenges. Seventy-three percent of the stepparents I surveyed said their faith was the biggest factor in the success of their stepparenting. Their relationship with God is what carried them through many storms. Jesus alludes to this strength in Luke 6 when He tells a parable about foundations. The house that was built on a strong faith was able to withstand the storm, but the one without it collapsed. Faith doesn't always determine success or failure in a stepfamily, but it gives you the added strength that many say is the reason they are able to survive.

I want to leave you with one more important statistic to include in this first chapter. Sixty-two percent of the stepparents I surveyed said their relationship with their stepchildren improved with time. The love and support you show your stepchild may not be reciprocated immediately, but one day your love will be seen from a different light. You may weather some storms as the child navigates his or her journey, but your consistent love and perseverance will eventually pay off.

Most stepparents concur that the story with stepchildren is a long one, and when you are in the middle of it, you sometimes feel as if you're at the end of your rope. If you stay the course, you will pass through the challenging chapters and get to a better place. If your stepchildren are ten or older, they probably won't start out by calling you the cookie lady and putting your arm around them at church. But if you persevere, even when you are a stepparent to older children, you may very well win a place in their heart. The "way in the wilderness" mentality helps you realize that your relationships are moving to a better place—and the journey takes time.

In Ephesians 3:16-20, Paul talks about a power that is available to us as stepparents. He says that God, through His Spirit, can do more within us than we can even imagine or possibly think. It is this power that gives you the strength to persevere in a task that may require more than you have. You will face challenges that require you to find support, and in the chapters that follow, I will talk about the help you can get to keep your family warm and strong. One thing is sure—you will experience both joy and pain being a stepparent, and you will learn more about God and yourself than you ever imagined. If you see your story through, you will also see God do things that seemed impossible.

No one may grow up dreaming of becoming a stepparent, but after ten years of actually doing it, I can say that I am grateful. God has used my stepparenting journey more than anything I've ever done to help me learn about His grace. As the years have passed, we have welcomed Jere's stepchildren and former in-laws into our family, and I have watched relationships grow and change in ways I never imagined. Some things are still a bit messy, but I've learned by experience to wait things out—anything can happen when you give it time. The more you open your heart, the bigger your family becomes.

Last year, Jere and I were having a dinner with our boy before he left for his summer trek to visit his mom in Australia. I was getting teary, and my now six-feet-two stepson came over to me, sat on my lap, and put his arms around me. He grabbed Jere's hand to join us, and I was suddenly transported back to that Sunday in church with much smaller arms and a less seasoned love. And though these moments of reflection are few and far between, I was silenced by the fullness of my heart.

I'm grateful to be secure enough with my stepson to be able to do this book together. I know his words at the end will help you understand a stepchild's perspective and will provide some wisdom from a different source. I am also grateful for the stepparents who opened up their struggles and experiences to lend their input to the following chapters. We need to know we are not alone and can gain from each other's wisdom and stories to help us make it through.

2

Party of Two—Plus One

(or Two or Three...)

Having a baby includes a pregnancy, doctor appointments, and classes to get you ready for the birth. When you become a stepparent, you have your wedding night and wake up with a child. No matter how much you prepare for it, instant parenthood can be a shock, especially if you have never been a parent before. Whether you are parenting full-time or half-time, acquiring an older child or one who needs full-time care, becoming a stepparent is like welcoming a new birth—except the child comes without the biology or shared history that normally helps you bond. Some people describe a stepparent as an "intimate stranger," and that is a good indicator of how you feel when you begin your role. Even if you had relationships with your stepchildren prior to marriage, they are suddenly related to you in a new way. They share your name and your home.

The morning after we returned from our honeymoon, I was in a haze of delirious bliss, and when I came around the corner and saw

Jordan standing there, I jumped. *You're still here!* I said (thankfully, not out loud). I had briefly forgotten that he had spent the night with us and would be waiting for me to feed him and help him get ready for school. I thought I had prepared myself for this new responsibility, but there is nothing like instant parenthood to remind you that life cannot be rehearsed. You just have to live the scene that is in front of you—and in my case, it was a six-year-old boy who needed breakfast and a ride to school.

Every stepparent faces some form of adjustment, ranging from a low-grade to a high-octane level, and it depends on the circumstances of your situation and the amount of time you are on duty. ("On duty" is code language for the period of time the child is living with you and you are responsible for full-time care.) Jordan's mom moved to Australia the first year of our marriage, so for me, motherhood suddenly escalated from half-time to full-time. There would be many more mornings getting ready for school, but I will never forget the first because that was when it hit me that for this period of time, this child was depending on me to take care of him. I was suddenly partly responsible for his growth and life. Though the responsibilities as a stepparent vary with the step-child's age, if you have custody of any children under eighteen, there will be a moment when you will be faced with the reality of parenting them. This can be especially daunting when your spouse is not home.

The school part I was down for—I strapped the car seat in my back seat, made my way through the carpool line, and even signed up to volunteer in Jordan's class once a week. Then I went to work, thankful my job at church had some flexibility for this new addition to my schedule. I'm embarrassed to admit the hardest part of the day was figuring out what I was going to do with him after I picked him up. This may be how parents feel when they are handed their first baby and are told to leave the hospital. I suspect some of them want to stay because they don't know how they are actually going to *do* it on their own. My husband worked from nine to five, and Jordan ended school at two-thirty, so it wouldn't be long before I was in charge.

Two-thirty came, and just before I picked up Jordan, I called my friend Cheryl. Cheryl had two kids in high school and a third Jordan's age, so I boldly invited myself over to her house. "Can Jordan and I come over for a playdate?" I asked her, trying to disguise the desperation in my voice. I eventually told her I was terrified and had no idea what I was doing, and that I needed some company to ease me into my new job as a mom. I figured if she was with me, and Jordan had someone fun to play with, I couldn't screw it up.

The kids played, we talked, and I asked her if we could move in. When you become a parent for the first time, you realize your need for support. This may be a good time to mention there are plenty of support groups for stepfamilies, and many of the stepparents who filled out my survey said that their support group was their saving grace. If you can't find one, you can always start one—there are probably other stepparents in your area who also could use some support. The important thing is that you find a place to vent and be understood. The frustrations and anxieties you will feel in your role are best expressed to others who can advise and support you in your challenges. Otherwise these frustrations can spill out onto your child, adding unneeded stress to the relationship you are trying to build.

Being a stepparent will often require you to put on your big-girl (or big-boy) pants. Whether you have to extend grace to a child who doesn't like or respect you, or relate to a biological parent who undermines your role, it takes maturity and intention to temper your emotions. Even in the best stepparenting situations, you will be called to exercise a maturity that your stepchild does not yet have.

The best thing I did when I became a stepparent was to find community to surround me. We all know it takes a village to raise a child (step or not), and having a solid community to parent within not only enriches your stepchild's life but also helps stabilize your new family. Our church community provided aunts, uncles, brothers, and sisters for Jordan to grow up with, and it allowed me to recruit experienced moms to have on call when I didn't have a clue what to do. Jordan is a different person because of the people around our family who became a part of his life. Suffice to say, the first thing to do as a new stepparent is to *get help*.

When I asked Cheryl if we could come over every day, she and I both knew that sooner or later I'd have to do afternoons with Jordan on my own. "You'll get it," she said. "I believe in you. You have been called to this. You may not feel equipped, but none of us do. You are the one called to come alongside this child and help him become who he's meant to be." Something about her words resonated deep in my soul. "Called" is a word that ignites you, perhaps terrifies you, and yet inspires you to face what is in front of you with a greater purpose. "God help me," I whimpered, and this became my most frequent prayer throughout my parenting. When I blew it, which I did frequently, Jordan never seemed to mind. We learned the dance of acceptance together. For older stepchildren, this dance takes longer and is often more complicated. For kids Jordan's age, they are mostly ready to embrace whatever love you have to give. The complications come later as they begin to navigate who they are.

When you are *called* to be a stepparent, your role is grounded in the belief that you were meant to be in your stepchild's life. This has been the secret sauce of my stepparenting, which has flourished because of my faith. The strength God gives us to undergird our sacrifices has been the reason I've been able to make it, and the belief that I am called to stepparenting has given me greater meaning than simply being a placeholder in Jordan's life. Affirming your calling will do the same for you.

BECOME A TWO FIRST

My faith has led me to find help from many insights from the Bible, and that has been a huge source of encouragement in my stepparenting journey. You will see some of those insights threaded throughout this book. The first verse I found that gave me unexpected insight into stepparenting was actually delivered in the middle of my wedding as

I took my vows: "Two are better than one, because they have a good return for their labor: If either of them falls down, one can help the other up. But pity anyone who falls and has no one to help them up" (Ecclesiastes 4:9-10).

When my friend Marlo read these words at the altar, I felt hot tears as I took in the enormity of what she was saying. I had chosen the passage, but the spoken power of the words caught me by surprise. When you spend half your life as a one, you'll never forget the moment you become a two. Soaking in the beauty of this verse, I inwardly celebrated what it would mean to finally be married. What I didn't know was how prophetic this verse would become for the task that lay ahead.

Presumably, you marry because you believe that you and your spouse will be better together. When your spouse has a child, you soon discover you have to live out this partnership in order to succeed. Your relationship with your spouse will be the make-or-break factor of your stepparenting. Author and fellow stepmother Wednesday Martin writes, "If you have stepchildren of any age, the most important person in your life is your husband. He is, quite simply, the person who in large part determines your happiness or misery in your step situation."[1] With the addition of clinging to God, I heartily agree with Ms. Martin's words.

Your spouse will not only broker your relationship with your stepchildren but also lay the path for your parenting. Your ability to communicate and stand together as a team will make the difference in how your parenting path is formed. As important as stepparenting is, what is more important is your relationship with each other. The problem is, it is easy to sacrifice growing in your marriage because your parenting challenges will have louder demands. Stepfamily expert Ron Deal adds to Ms. Martin's words when he writes, "It's easy for your marriage to get lost in the stepfamily forest, and without a strong marriage your entire family falls apart."[2] Whether the research comes from a secular or Christian source, the advice is the same: Your number one priority as a stepparent is your relationship with your spouse. Read that again.

Focusing on your marriage may seem like a strange priority when you suddenly have a stepchild in your care. But your marriage will determine the way your relationship with your stepchild forms. Your spouse needs to be as committed to your stepparenting as you are. The intimacy and communication you develop together will enrich your parental bond. James Bray, a leading stepfamily researcher, says that "marital satisfaction almost always determines stepfamily stability."[3] It's as simple as this: The more you grow as a couple, the stronger your stepparenting will be. Your spouse will be the one to present you, support you, and defend you to your stepchild. You are entering an already formed relationship between your spouse and your child that is established and strong. Your ability to communicate your feelings, needs, and challenges to your spouse can make the difference in whether or not you survive.

Jere and I had regular date nights apart from Jordan to grow in our relationship. We talked about the challenges and emotions we each felt and communicated the struggles from our vantage points so we could work together. The varied and ever-changing dynamics in our home made it imperative for us to function as a team. When you are a new stepparent, if you aren't able to communicate to your spouse your needs and feelings, they can end up spilling out on your stepchildren in ways you regret. Unspoken tension in your home can make you feel overwhelmed and alone. One stepparent on my survey sadly articulated her lack of support with this one piece of advice to prospective stepparents: "Don't become one. It's the hardest thing I've ever done." Making the effort to grow from "I" to "we" in your marriage can make the difference and even determine whether your stepfamily survives.

My story and every study I read affirms that your spouse is the key to your stepparenting success. The more your spouse does to establish and support you as a co-parent, the more solid your stepfamily will be—even if the children don't accept you at first. Ron Deal wisely suggests that stepfamilies are cooked in Crock-Pots, not microwaves, and the time you take to establish and strengthen your home by becoming a team with your spouse will reap dividends in the future. Your spouse establishes your position by standing by your side in your parenting, and you make it easier on your spouse by not making them choose between you and their child. Taking the time to learn to communicate with each other will help you stand together as a parenting team.

As a stepparent, you have much to add to the parenting process because you have an objectivity the biological parent doesn't have. If you operate with the Crock-Pot mentality in carving out your place, you will eventually be a unique voice of love in your stepchild's life. Because of the upheaval that brought your stepfamily together, it will take time and consistency to establish yourself as a parent. You may have to weather a season of testing, but if you hold firm in your resolve to love your child, your effort will eventually pay off. The trust and commitment and teamwork you build with your spouse paves the way for you to persevere in your role.

In a study of two hundred stepfamilies, James Bray discovered that a stepfamily is at greatest risk during the first two years.[4] This statistic is opposite from first marriages, which often start out well and decline with the hardships that come. The positive news is that if you can make it through the first two years as a stepfamily, you will be stronger than most couples in first marriages. You will also have a better chance at navigating the difficulties and challenges ahead. Everything you do the first two years to build into your marriage is an investment that will pay off—not only for you but also for your children. Not only will it help you establish a foundation that is secure enough to weather your parenting storms, it will also allow you to work together to bring your stepchild into your marriage to find his place.

THE BIRTH OF THE SANDWICH

When Jere and I told Jordan we were engaged, we spontaneously put him between us for a hug, and one of us yelled out "Sandwich!" It was one of those times when a word pops out of your mouths and somehow sticks. "Sandwich" became the perfect way to show Jordan he had a secure place in our marriage and life. We knew he was probably figuring out what it would mean to share his beloved daddy, and we wanted him to know I was another layer of parenting to surround him. Since he was six years old, "sandwich" was the perfect terminology to communicate in a way he understood. As we started bonding together as a family, this metaphor assured him that he would always be in the middle of the mix.

Whether we were at a movie, sitting at the table, or lounging on the couch, we made the effort to position Jordan between us. Much to his teenage chagrin now when he watches our wedding video, we even lodged him between us during our first dance. We wanted him to feel right from the start that my intent was never to stand between him and his dad. The sandwich gave us a symbol that let him know he would always be a part of what we were together.

Let me be clear that I don't recommend using this metaphor if you are called to parent adolescents. Telling teenagers that you are all going to be a sandwich might inspire them to let you know they would rather be open-faced. But if you are coming into stepparenting with younger kids, I share this metaphor as something to have in front of you. Your spouse's children may not verbalize it, but they are likely wondering what their place will be now that you are part of their family life. This is also true for older kids, but keep the metaphors to yourself, and recognize your bonding needs to happen more slowly. Anything you do to show your stepkids that your intention is not to stand between them and your spouse will help them see you as less of a threat. Our "sandwich" provided a way for Jordan to see his dad and me united in our love for him and to begin to experience our parenting as a team.

When you have multiple stepchildren and/or biological children, "sandwich" may not be the best word to describe what you have. The point is not to stuff the kids into your perfect picture of a family, but to keep your stepchildren prominently in the mix. Knowing that your stepchildren are dealing with insecurity (even if they don't show it) helps you find ways to give them reassurance (even if they act like they don't need it). The time and care you give to include them strengthens not only your relationship with them but also the relationship you are building with your spouse. Loving your spouse's children is one of the strongest ways to build your marriage.

When you are called to marry a parent, you will often need to prioritize the kids who come with your marriage. You may sacrifice some things as a newlywed, but the sacrifices you make to include your spouse's children actually bond you closer with your spouse. Your love for your stepchildren will look different depending on their age and acceptance and the pace they are comfortable with. At first, that love may not be returned the way you wish it would be. But if you stand with your spouse in loving your stepchildren, the two of you will inevitably grow closer with this shared goal.

Having a sandwich mentality not only helped us in the time we spent with Jordan, it also helped us with decisions we made apart from him. We thought about his needs even while we were away meeting our own. When Jere and I went on dates, we brought good people into Jordan's community. We found a couple of college students who could consistently spend time with him, and as time went on, he was as excited about them coming as we were about going on our date. They grew to love Jordan in a special way, and to this day, they still keep in touch and track his growth. They became a part of his village and gave us the important gift of building our marriage.

We also had extended "couple time" when Jordan went to be with his mom in Australia. But even during the seven weeks when he wasn't with us, we found ways to let him know that our sandwich was missing him and that we were excited to welcome him back. At times, other parents envied our childless vacation, but the tradeoff was the emptiness we felt when he left us. It was a reminder that he didn't belong only to us. Our sandwich had to stretch to include the layers of Jordan's other life.

Your stepchild has two homes, and as warm and wonderful as you make yours, you are only half his story. Helping your child come and go as comfortably and easily as possible helps him navigate his divided life. This mentality helps you prepare for your children's departure as well as their reentry. It empowers you to hold space in your heart and home while they are gone and prepares you to accommodate their transition when they come back. Stepchildren don't ask to have two homes, and this juggling back and forth alters their lives forever because of a decision that was made for them. This juggling will be especially tough for them in younger years because routine breeds security, and their routine changes depending on where they spend the night. Your flexibility to help them transition as easily as possible in their coming and going is a gift you give their hearts.

James Bray's study found that a solid and loving stepfamily can actually help heal the scars of divorce. So the commitment you make to love your stepchild may actually help to repair your child's heart. For the first three years of our marriage, Jordan asked me to lie next to him at bedtime so he would be able to sleep better. I knew there was something deeper going on, and I was honored to be part of the healing that was taking place. Bray's study of stepfamilies affirmed that a loving stepfamily that functions well can restore a child's sense of emotional and psychological well-being.[5] You can be part of that healing if you are willing to love your stepchildren through the brokenness that occurred in their family whether they want you to or not.

If your stepchild is a teenager, your support will probably look different than mine did with Jordan. Now that he is a teenager, I look back on those cuddle times wistfully, as they have been replaced with rolled eyes and grunts. Your commitment to love in whatever way your stepchildren allow will contribute to the healing they may need. One parent on my survey wrote, "When you love your stepchild unconditionally, even if the child doesn't respond to it, he will notice." It may take months or years, but you could very well be the one God will use to help mend their wounded heart. With so many difficulties stacked up against stepparenting, this can motivate us to persevere in this daunting task.

CRYING FOR KAYA

"Who is Kaya?" I whispered to my husband as Jordan dissolved into tears. He had seen a dog on television, and it sent him into an emotional response that was much bigger than the show. We held him close and waited till he stopped. When we were out of his room, I waited to hear about Kaya and how close he must have been to our sweet boy.

Jere looked puzzled. "Kaya was our family dog. Jordan spent very little time with him." We were both struck by the largeness of Jordan's response. There was clearly a deeper reason why he wept.

During the first two years of my stepparenting, there were sporadic times when Jordan grieved his family's separation. I came to realize he was grieving a loss he only subconsciously knew. The family dog represented life with his mom and dad, and even though he was very young when they separated, crying for Kaya was one of the ways he grieved their separation. Each time he mentioned Kaya, instead of minimizing it or wondering why it happened out of the blue, we just held him and said we understood. And one day he didn't cry for Kaya anymore.

The first year of your marriage as a stepparent includes grieving and loss for what transpired before you. That is not anyone's dream for beginning a life together, but it is a reality you must contend with if you want your stepfamily to heal and thrive. Most stepchildren are not consciously aware of their grieving and will act out in different ways depending on their age and circumstances. When Jordan cried for a dog he barely knew, I was tempted to rescue his tears with logic, wanting him to "feel better" and not be so sad. But we learned to hold him while he cried and to trust this was part of the process of Jordan acclimating to his new and divided life.

This grieving may take shape in different ways, but all stepfamilies experience it. Though it boils up through different behavior, your awareness of it gives you an understanding and empathy that helps you absorb (and occasionally deflect) what doesn't belong to you. A six-year-old's tears present a much more appealing package than a teenager's rudeness or cruelty. Both are evidence of grief for a child's divided family, and you may bear the brunt of that grief.

The gift and challenge of being a stepparent is that you have the opportunity to fill some of the holes left by divorce in your stepchild's life. But you may have to look past the surface of your stepchild's behavior to see what is really there. Whether your child is six or sixteen, seeing past their words and actions to their wounds helps you meet whatever behavior you encounter. And whether the child's grief manifests in tears, anger, or a barrage of stories that don't include you, knowing you can be part of your child's healing gives you the motivation you need to stand in the gap with your grace.

Remember that in the first years of your marriage, you are not anywhere near the end of the story. Having the long view gives you the perspective to endure what might be happening now. As one stepparent on my survey said, "This is a marathon, not a sprint, and it takes more time than you think you need." It's that Crock-Pot mentality that helps you persevere and know your story isn't through.

OTHER PACKAGES OF GRIEF

"Tell the story of when you and Mom were on your honeymoon… when you did stand-up comedy in the van with Dan Rowan, and everyone thought you were friends." One prompt like that was all my dad needed to start. Storytelling was his specialty, and he loved nothing more than entertaining us for hours with stories from the past. This was especially true when his stories included a brush with fame, and meeting Dan Rowan (from the old show *Rowan & Martin's Laugh-In*) was one of his favorite ones to tell. My dad's new wife sat silently as my brothers and I egged him on… and happily left her out. This pattern was repeated at countless dinner conversations and family get-togethers. I'm embarrassed to admit the deep satisfaction I felt every time he launched in about our old life.

I don't think I purposely wanted my new stepmom to be left out of our conversation. But I obviously felt a deep need to be connected to the part of my life that I had lost with my parents' divorce. Getting my dad to tell stories of our past was my way of bringing up the memories of nineteen years of my childhood. Only now as a stepmother myself do I feel what my stepmother must have felt at those dinnertime talks. Her graciousness to allow us to press on in conversations and stories that didn't include her showed me her willingness to stand in the gap during our transition and let us heal.

Grief comes in many packages, and when I egged my dad to retell our memories, it was coming from my feelings of loss. What took shape in Jordan's crying for Kaya reared its head in my prompting my dad to tell stories—and it will likely take shape in another way altogether when it comes to your stepkids and you. The point is to recognize grief and loss when it happens. It is what you walked into, and sometimes you may be called to absorb what doesn't belong to you.

Looking back on my own experience as an adult stepchild, I now see my behavior with my stepmom with more mature eyes. I understand how she must have felt because of my stepparent perspective, and I see more clearly how she had to wade through her personal discomfort as our family divided and healed. This discomfort took shape in a much different way from what I experienced with Jordan, but it represented the same adjustment that every stepfamily requires. You are coming into a story that has been going on before you, and you will need to make room for your family's previous story as you make your way into it.

It's been thirty-six years since my stepmother entered our family. It's been eleven years since I married Jordan's dad. The time that has passed has helped me to see that what happens at the beginning of stepparenting is part of a longer story that will unfold. However, the beginning of the story is important—it lays the foundation for the relationships you will develop and grow in the time to come.

Stepparenting is a marathon, not a sprint, and the first few years will demand you accommodate people's grief and feelings. There will be pain and joy as you become an indelible part of your stepchild's life. The long view of stepparenting will help you live this beginning chapter as best you can, knowing this is not the way the story will always be. But the way you love your child in the first years of your parenting sets the course for how it unfolds.

With support from God and your spouse, you can be equipped to carry this burden. It is also incredibly important to remember that the burden will shift and change and that you will have a different role someday. As your stepfamily grows and develops, your children will grow too, and eventually they will realize what they can't see right now about you and their family. And if you persevere in your love, one day the stories told about your family will include you.

3

Making Room

When I became a stepmom, I discovered that I harbored an aversion to the term. This became apparent to me when I had trouble getting the word "stepmom" out of my mouth. Saying the word seemed to advertise to others that I was not the real mom—that I was second place in the food chain of moms, even though being one took up 80 percent of my job description. It also felt like it carried a different undertone than adoptive mom and slapped me with "unpopular add-on" status as soon as it came out of my mouth. I had no trouble being a stepmom. I just didn't care to have the name that came with it.

The stepmother is the character you never want to be in fairytales—unless you want to play the villain. She is threatening or even downright wicked—sometimes even a desperate seductress. She is the one you want to get rid of to get to your happy end. The truth is, I felt embarrassed by the label, so I made peace with the term by simply avoiding it. I never lied about it—I just never offered it up.

Because my husband and I had primary custody and Jordan's mom lived in another country, many people assumed I was Jordan's biological mom. This was an impression I neither fed nor lied about, but I noticed I never interrupted people to announce that I was the stepmom instead. This inward observation made me aware of two things: The term carried a stigma I would need to reimagine, and I would eventually need to humbly accept what I actually was. I loved being Jordan's second mom—I just had to get over the hump of bearing the name that came with it. But here's what is most important: Affirming that I was Jordan's stepmom made room for the mom who preceded me in his life.

In most stepparenting situations, declaring that you are the stepmom isn't a big deal because everyone around you already knows it. However, in my situation, it was the way I made room for Jordan's mom when she wasn't there. Whether your child's biological parent is next door, in another country, or out of the picture altogether, part of the call of being a stepparent is to respect and recognize the biological parent's place in your stepchild's life. Even if you are in that rare situation that allows you to gloss over it or discount it, your child's healthy development will partly depend on your ability to make room for the biological parent's place. It also helps you remember yours.

Because of my age when I married, along with my husband's predetermined condition (translation: vasectomy), we decided not to pull out all the stops to try to have a child. Instead, we made it our focus to raise the child he already had. So part of my process was making peace that being Jordan's stepmom was all the mother I was going to be.

Whether you have biological children or not, becoming a stepparent invites you to play a unique role in a child's life. It is more than a throwaway position you tolerate while you focus on your relationship with your spouse or raising your own kids. You have the privilege of standing in the gap for a child who isn't yours, for the sake of helping him thrive after his parents' divorce. Even if your unconditional love is not initially reciprocated, it can help change your child's life. And with this calling comes the ability to accommodate your parenting to make room for the biological parent in your stepchild's life.

The place of your biological counterpart in your stepfamily is something all stepparents need to negotiate. Whether you are faced with this immediately at the beginning of your marriage or come to grips with it as you go, the biological parent is part of the package your spouse and stepchild bring to your life. My challenges with Jordan's mom have been harder in my heart than my schedule because mothering Jordan is a huge part of my identity. Because we parent independently (and far away from each other) and I have no other children, it has been easy (and extremely tempting) for me to slip into the perceived role of being Jordan's only mom. But with the extraordinary gift I've been given, I've had to pry my hands open from clinging to him and remember my place in parenting him. Embracing the shared package Jordan came in helps me live my calling best, and my willingness to do so helps him thrive.

As Jordan grows older, my husband and I have been more consistently aware that we are only half of his story. Since we've parented so far away from his mom in Australia, it has taken time to really feel what has always been there. We have seen evidence of his other side reflected in his biology, and he is connected in a more ongoing way to his mom because of his age and continuing advances in technology. After he graduates high school, his connection to Australia could be a part of himself he'll want to explore. You may face the awareness of your child's other side much earlier in your stepparenting if you share custody more frequently and don't parent your child for long stretches. But whether you are faced with accommodating your child's biological parent right up front or as time moves on, your maturity to step back and make room for that parent allows your child to sift through all the parts of himself. Working toward as much peace and unity as you can to make this possible is one of the greatest ways to love your child. It will also have the spiritual side effect of growing grace in you.

THE CALLING YOU HAVE RECEIVED

"I urge you to live a life worthy of the calling you have received. Be completely humble and gentle; be patient, bearing with one another in love. Make every effort to keep the unity of the Spirit through the bond of peace" (Ephesians 4:1-3).

I don't believe Paul was thinking of stepparenting when he wrote these words from prison. However, the words he uses fit perfectly (and sometimes painfully) for those of us who marry someone with a child. You will be called to lay down your rights, alter your schedule, and possibly face unearned criticism that may drive you into a private room to scream. Keeping your eyes on the importance of what you are participating in will give you the impetus to stay the course.

Ron Deal suggests that as your stepfamily develops, you will need to separate the personal from the parental. A thousand emotions and reactions will happen between you, your spouse, and your spouse's ex, and they may need to be subdued and overlooked. On top of that, you will have your own feelings and frustrations that may need to be aired to a trusted friend or therapist so they don't spill into your stepparenting. Forging bonds with your spouse, your stepchild, and the biological parent becomes even more complicated when you bring your own stuff into the mix. There is no way to pull off gentleness and humility if you are angry in your marriage or overwhelmed in your parenting. Getting help outside your home will help you be the healthiest you can be as you tackle this assignment.

Any maturity and restraint you can show will be a gift you give your character as well as your stepchild. The situation will likely grow less volatile with time because of the trust and confidence your caring will eventually win. Your husband's ex may never cheer for you, but your commitment to love her child will speak volumes in the long run of your stepfamily. Let this hope carry you through what she might think or say about you when you first begin.

You are walking into a divorce that separated two people in marriage but left them joined together in child rearing. That adds a third party to your marriage and makes you a third party to what is left from theirs. There is no way to fully prepare for all the ways this will stretch your heart. You may absorb emotions from your biological counterpart that aren't personal to you but come from residue that exists between her and your spouse. You are also going to be overly (and sometimes unfairly) scrutinized because of the weighty position you now have in her child's life. Understanding the fear behind words or behavior that may feel cruel or unfair helps you deflect what doesn't belong to you. She does not know yet who you are and has an understandable concern for what your parenting will mean for her child.

I stumbled across a website called Stepmomming that gave some great advice for beginning a relationship with a biological parent. Kristen, the stepmother who hosts this site, suggests making a date with the biological parent to tell her more about who you are and the commitment you want to make to her and her child. In her experience, taking this initiative caused her biological parent counterpart to accept and even grow to honor her place as a supportive parent. However, this kind of meeting includes brokering a relationship with your spouse's ex that you may not have the freedom or ability to begin. My personal experience is that if you aren't able to communicate your intentions directly, you can reveal your commitment and character through your actions and responses. Going into this delicate relationship with the knowledge that you will weather some discomfort will equip you to respond with the humility and patience Paul suggests. There is also no substitute for time in establishing your credibility for who you are.

The ability to look behind the words and actions of the people in your stepfamily is a skill you need in successful stepparenting. It will help you see past a volatile situation with a biological parent, and it will empower you to understand the way your child might behave. It will also give you grace for some of the behavior you see in yourself. You will not always respond perfectly, and that is why no one writes a book on perfect stepparenting. This book is about grace-filled stepparenting, and while you are extending it to everyone around you, make sure to include yourself.

It may be helpful to know that stepfamily experts say the "settling in" period for a remarriage is five to seven years. Sometimes when things are more complicated, it can last up to twelve years.[1] That means that the entire time your stepchild is growing up and spending time in your house, you may never feel settled in. You just make room for unsettledness and get used to it until your children are raised and gone. As a stepparent, you are not in this for a sprint. There will be difficult chapters to bear, knowing that the story of your stepfamily isn't through. Someday you'll see more things come together than you do right now in your stepparenting. All the humility, gentleness, and patience that you can possibly muster as things are shifting and settling will reap dividends in your stepfamily's life.

To "make every effort to keep the unity," you may have to remember that you are only half of the parenting story. You will never control what others say or do, but you have the power to determine your response. This is a power you want to grab on to as a stepparent, because you have very little control over many things that happen to you and around you. My planning personality took many hits when I became a stepparent, and I quickly discovered the only plan that works is to be prepared at all times to abandon the plan. That might be the best piece of advice for any stepparent, no matter what your situation may be. You will never completely own your schedule, your child's discipline, or your parenting plan, and this unfortunately begins the moment the honeymoon ends. You married someone who brought the need for flexibility into your life. Humility, gentleness, and patience are three quiet forces that will enable you to find your stride.

When two people have a child, they never fully end their relationship. So depending on the state of the relationship between your spouse and your biological counterpart, the beginning of your marriage may be a minefield of emotions that you need to broker for the sake of the child you now share. Keeping humility, gentleness, and patience in front of you as you participate in all sorts of uncomfortable situations will help you survive the initial stages. The alternatives of anger, insecurity, and pride may be easier to access, but those are the responses you want to subdue. In the first few years of stepparenting, choosing Paul's words will set you on a better course.

CO-PARENTING, PARALLEL
PARENTING, AND WINGING IT
WITH WHAT YOU'VE GOT

Somewhere between taking my blood pressure and grabbing his stethoscope, my doctor looked up and casually began talking about his family. Looking relaxed and tanned, he mumbled something about recently returning from a vacation in Hawaii with his wife and ex-wife. My face must have betrayed my curiosity because he went on to describe his blended family. He and his ex parented their kids together—with the help of his current wife—and they vacationed yearly as one big bunch. While he talked, I gazed at a family photo and decided not to mention that it looked like an episode of *Sister Wives*. He had been able to achieve a model of co-parenting that looked amazingly cozy, and while it must have been great for the kids, I couldn't help but feel awkward imagining a vacation with Jere, his ex, and me.

I had seen a flash of this kind of co-parenting in the movie *Stepmom*, when Isabel (Julia Roberts) and Jackie (Susan Sarandon) came together after Jackie got cancer. I had also seen a glimpse of it in *People* magazine where two "uncoupled" exes formed a liaison with new partners in raising their kids.[2] My doctor was the first example I saw in real life. You may be one of the rare stepparents who has this kind of connection, but most stepfamilies don't look like this. You just work with what you've got and make it as comfortable as you can for your kids.

Our stepparenting arrangement is not vindictive or hateful, but I would say it falls short of blissfully harmonious. I can say we've evolved in our stepfamily to a much better place with time. There have been times when we've negotiated awkward conversations and value differences, and "cooperative co-parenting" doesn't exactly describe the way our parenting styles meshed during those seasons. I would describe it as two families each having a hand in parenting Jordan as they live separate lives. I was relieved when I read Wednesday Martin's words that "if cooperative co-parenting is the ideal, parallel parenting is the norm." She cites Mavis Hetherington's study, in which half of the divorced parents she had tracked evolved into an arrangement of more or less ignoring each other and letting each other do his or her own thing. In parallel parenting, communication between the couples is minimal and mostly related to logistics. The child learns to acclimate to the rules and behavior of each home.[3] While not as ideal as cooperative co-parenting, researchers found that hearing "This is how we do things here" a couple of times was enough to help kids transition between their two homes.

We don't totally ignore each other, but I suppose you could say we let each other do our own thing. Studies have shown that only a small percentage of divorced parents achieve cooperative co-parenting; many formerly married couples settle for parallel parenting in an effort to make peace. This was the arrangement I walked into, and it allowed us to raise Jordan mostly the way we wanted to during the nine months he was with us. It also meant we let go of having input in his other family and let them do the same.

The difference in our styles and values surfaced most when Jordan traveled back and forth between us. We handled this transition by making room for the differences of Jordan's other life while not compromising his life with us. We discovered the best way to do that was to plan activities right after he came home with the community he was a part of here so he'd remember the parts of himself he had forgotten. Rather than spend our time repeating "That's not how we do things here," we wanted him to experience the faith and influence of our community in more positive, less critical ways. For that reason, we took the time to plan experiences where he could be around people living out their faith rather than telling him what not to say or do.

Whether that took shape in a mission trip, a camp, or a family vacation with friends, this transition strategy worked well in our parallel parenting arrangement. It allowed us not to criticize Jordan's other family or their influence while we stood fast with what we believed to be important for his life. As he grew older, I came to realize that juggling between our two families created a need for him to develop two ways of being that he learned to accommodate. This is a burden we wish he didn't have to carry, but it comes from the differences in his two parents and the way we think, believe, and live our lives. Children of divorce have to negotiate this tension between their families, and the best you can do is give them freedom and grace as they transition between you. The circumstances of your stepfamily require you to let go of having control of all their influences and to trust God with their lives.

Being a child of a divorce is similar to having citizenship in two countries.[4] In our situation, this is literally true, but it is also symbolic of the transition Jordan has to make. As he travels back and forth between our families, he must adjust to customs, values, and differences that require him to acclimate. The amiable relationship between our "countries" allows Jordan to travel back and forth in peace. While we are different, we respect each other's way of doing things for the sake of Jordan's well-being. Jere and I have made a rule that we never speak critically about Jordan's other family or their decisions, because to do so would create a conflict inside him that he shouldn't have to bear. If we are struggling with something, we wait until we are alone to talk, and this is one rule we've worked hard to keep. Words you speak out loud can never be unsaid, regardless of how much you wish you could take them back.

Researcher James Bray confirms that when one parent speaks negatively about another parent, the child internalizes the comment.[5] Your child may choose to defend or harbor the comment, but you are handing him a burden you have the power to relieve. You feel great tension when the stakes are high, and you worry that a value you hold dear is being compromised. You will have to trust that the way you live and your influence in your child's life are worth more than any words you could say. Someday Jordan will make decisions of his own about what he believes and how he lives, and he will choose the behavior and faith that fits for him. Until then, making room for the other part of his life allows him to embrace both of his families and ultimately make his own choice.

MAKING ROOM IN SCHEDULES

As I mentioned before, flexibility is the key to stepparenting success. The problem is, flexibility happens to be one trait I missed when they were being handed out. God has used stepparenting to softly shove this characteristic into my life. If you don't have it, chances are it will be shoved into yours. Whether it's making room in your schedule for unplanned changes or accommodating a different attitude when your child returns to your home, your flexibility will pave the way to much smoother stepparenting. Otherwise, you can count on some rocky times.

Two months after our wedding, a devastating earthquake shattered Port Au Prince, Haiti, and a dear friend of mine is a pastor there. He was one of the pastors who married us, and he was in the heart of the devastation when it hit. He came inches away from his own death, was separated from his children for several days, and had to support many people in his church who were homeless. Because I had known and supported Ephraim for fifteen years, Jere and I decided to go as soon as it was safe to assess the damage and find out how we could help. He and his family were close to both our hearts, so we wanted to see what his needs were and bring back news to caring friends so they could know how to support him. We checked our custody schedule and purchased two nonrefundable tickets during a time when Jordan would be in Australia with his mom. Imagine my delight when the schedule changed and we learned he was coming back while we were gone.

I'd love to say that I happily rearranged our plan to accommodate this news and gained big points as a new stepparent. The truth is, I fought back by countering that we had already purchased tickets within our custody arrangement, and therefore we should be able to hold the plan we already had in place. You can guess how well that conversation went. This was the first time I discovered that "oughts" and "shoulds" are best left out of parallel parenting relationships.

As it worked out, a wonderful friend stayed with Jordan so we could go ahead with the three-day trip as planned.

I'm happy to say that ten years later, Jordan's mom and I are much more communicative about plans in advance and do our best to accommodate each other. I only tell you this story because it was the first time I remember understanding the power of my response. Ramping up and fighting back is not a strategy I recommend for developing peace in your stepfamily arrangement. When it comes to schedules and parenting, there will be times when you will be asked (or told) to sacrifice plans you've made, and you may feel like you are losing ground. Oddly, your willingness to accommodate your biological counterpart's schedule can actually have the opposite effect. Whether it's having to cancel something you were looking forward to or making room for an unwelcome change, your willingness to accommodate will bring more peace to your relationship. Knowing it is a season that will not go on forever gives you the strength to function in this season in a way you won't regret.

One parent on my survey advised, "Be willing to put up with difficult situations when you can't affect them." Whether it is accommodating a biological parent's sudden change, or acquiring a financial responsibility that takes you off guard, this advice is brilliant and sound. If you are generally a responder, you will have an easier time acquiescing to changing schedules. If you are a planner (or less attractively, a controller) like me, you may kick and scream but will hopefully be wise enough to give in. You will never regret making concessions for the greater good of your child. That's the big picture of what you are fighting for, and sometimes you need to lose a battle in order to win the war.

No matter how happy you feel going into your marriage, shared parenting can add difficulty and stress you never would have imagined. But if you see your marriage and stepparenting as a calling, you are motivated by something more than your personal happiness and getting your own needs met. Calling carries you when you have to cancel that romantic trip because of the other parent's sudden change in schedule. The precious life in your care is worth a thousand romantic trips. (Just be sure to reschedule it. Soon.)

BEING CALLED MOM

"Mom, will you help me?" I heard a voice softly say through the crack of his bedroom door, and my heart skipped a beat. I wanted to hold it in the air, even if it was unintentional, because it was so natural and unforced. I took note of the swelling inside my soul as I walked in his room, trying to act unphased. I didn't want to move what had happened from its unforced place.

Jere and I were a few months into our marriage when Jordan took this leap in our relationship. Some stepparents never are called Mom or Dad because of the age of the children they are called to parent or how late they come into the children's lives. Jordan called me Mom largely because he was six years old and because I was blessed to be given a lot of time with him. But this leap meant we would need to reconcile how to accommodate the feelings of the mom he already had.

We had settled on "Laurie Mom" when we first got married, but the phrase was long and cumbersome. He often shortened it to Laurie, and even though it felt awkward when I volunteered in his second-grade class, I wanted him to be able to take our relationship at his pace.

When "Mom" slipped out, I suspected it might be a significant transition. In order to make room for how Jordan might feel about his loyalty to his biological mom, we agreed that Jere should have a conversation with him to explore his feelings without me there.

Our geography made our parenting situation slightly unique in that Jordan's mom and I were rarely together except in passing. Mostly Jordan traveled between us and had just one mom wherever he was. When Jere talked to him, he discovered Jordan had come up with his own plan for how to address me. He said when his mom from Australia was present, she would be the only one he would call Mom. However, when he was away from her, and over here with me, he would like to call me Mom, because it was easier. He's held to that plan ever since.

Being called Mom or Dad as a stepparent can range from being no big deal to a biological parent all the way up to divisive. Some biological parents don't care whether their child extends this name to a stepparent, and others care very deeply, so you will need to negotiate how this will play out. As time has passed, Jordan's mom has come to know and trust me more, and our arrangement of toggling back and forth with the name Mom seems to work for our situation. Like many biological parents, she initially did not want him to call me that, and his plan allowed him to respect her desire. After ten years of parenting, sharing this name seems more benign than it used to be. But when we are all together, supporting Jordan to give her the name exclusively is one way to put her comfort over my own.

Sometimes I wish my heart was bigger when she visits here and I hear him call me Laurie. But I know it's one small way I make room for the presence and place Jordan's mom has in his life. It has also taught me that what your stepchild calls you is incidental to your relationship. You don't want to be overly focused on orchestrating what he or she calls you and miss being engaged in their relationship with you. Enjoy and appreciate whatever your stepchild gives you and recognize there are things happening now that will form the path of what your relationship becomes. You may never have "Mom" or "Dad" grace your ears, but that won't change your impact on them. Who you are is more important than what you are called.

Your stepchild will set the pace of intimacy, and your job is to be there to respond to it. Your spouse will broker your connection initially, but soon you'll have your own relationship with your stepchild that will deepen with time. Many stepparents don't have as much time with their stepchild as I do, and I am grateful to Jordan's mom for the place in his life her circumstances allowed me to have. But with this gift comes the requirement to hold Jordan loosely, and I am aware how quickly I can move from grateful to possessive. Stepparenting is a gift from God that comes with instructions to hold your stepchild with open hands.

When two families are raising a child, they must face insecurities, deal with different personalities, and make room for unshared values. Even stepfamilies like my doctor's (or pictured in *People* magazine) carry emotions and tensions we may not see or hear anything about. The best way to approach stepparenting is to do what it takes to love your child and make ample room for the biological parent who preceded you. She or he is going through just as much—if not more—when it comes to making room for you in her child's life.

4

The Weight of Influence

Jere and I were flying through movie choices one evening when we settled on *Three Identical Strangers*, a documentary about three men who had never met but discovered they were triplets. Documentaries do not usually get voted on when we have a movie night, but the story of how these three brothers found each other drew us in. The reunion occurred in 1980, and when the story first hit the press, it seemed to support biology as the biggest influential factor in a child's development. At the time, psychiatrists were split on whether nature or nurture had the greatest influence on development. But watching these boys' mannerisms after so many years of being apart seemed to leave no doubt. They amazed television audiences with their uncanny similarities and remarkable reunion story.

They had been fortuitously reunited when one of the boys arrived at college and people waved and smiled as if they knew him. Strangers started calling him by another name, and he knew he was being mistaken for someone else. When someone on campus arranged a meeting between him and his "twin," the extraordinary story began to unfold.

A third young man saw the estranged twins' faces in the news and was compelled by their similar appearance to meet them. The three brothers had each been adopted separately, but after all these years, they all looked and acted eerily alike.

What made the story interesting was that the adoption agency had not told the adoptive families that they had adopted one of three triplets. A psychiatrist named Peter Neubauer worked with the agency to keep the boys' biological ties hidden so he could study how nurture and nature impacted their growth. Their reunion revealed such incredible similarities that at first, it seemed clear that nature had the dominant influence. But in the last few minutes of the film, their story revealed significant differences in the boys' trajectories, and it became clear that nurture had also played a part. Because of this twist, the highly unethical experiment revealed that both biology and environment had contributed to who these boys became.

The nature-nurture battle has continued throughout time, mostly with a truce, as the forces appear to be equal. Multiple studies have set out to prove the superiority of one or the other, but recent research says they intersect equally in determining who a person ultimately becomes.[1] Understanding the power of nurture helps you realize the potential influence you will have in your stepchild's growth and development. Conversely, understanding the power of nature helps you make room for your stepchild's biology, which will also be a significant part of who he or she becomes. You may not share your child's biology, but because you are one of the parents in your stepchild's life, you *will* have an influence on his or her development. At every stage of influence—whether you are functioning more like a coach, a friend, or a parent—you have a stake in your stepchild's growth. Your relationship with your stepchild may not be as close as you want, but if you focus on the relationship you have, you will discover there are always opportunities to contribute to your stepchild's development. And as your relationship evolves, your influence in your stepchild's life may grow to be more than you imagined it could be.

BEGIN WITH YOU

From the start of your relationship, you can influence your stepchild through your example. In fact, it's fair to say if your stepchild lives with you at least part-time, you *will* influence him, whether you are doing it intentionally or not. This can be scary to think about, but it can also be empowering as you consider your role as a stepparent. It also takes your focus off your stepchild and helps you look at something you *can* control—you.

Faith is more caught than taught, so if you and your spouse are living out values that reflect a relationship with God, your stepchild will notice. In our home, that doesn't mean perfect behavior (which never happens), but apologizing when we've blown it, and letting Jordan see our commitment to God when things are hard. In 2 Timothy 1:5, Paul affirms that Timothy's sincere faith first lived in the people who raised him and taught him. Because you are half of your stepchild's family, you and your spouse have the opportunity to do the same.

The way you live, struggle, make decisions, and treat each other will speak more to your stepchildren than anything you teach them. The faith that lives in you can grow to live in them, and you may be a significant part of God's plan to reach them because you share a home. Part of your calling is to live your life in front of your stepchild, and this is something to consider apart from your relationship with him. It causes you to focus less on what your stepchild is doing and concentrate more on what your stepchild sees in you. This is the only part of your stepparenting you can control.

When you begin with yourself, you'll feel more empowered in your stepparenting. Instead of being a victim to your stepchild's behavior, you can consciously hold the power of your response. As a stepparent, think of yourself less like a thermometer and more like a thermostat. Rather than letting your circumstances with your stepchildren move you up and down, you can set the temperature of your home. With the chaos your stepchildren may experience as they transition back and forth between two families, your stability and dependability will be comforting to them. Your stepchild may go through many different emotions and stages with you, but if you stay secure in who you are, you will provide a steady framework for your stepfamily to grow.

Perhaps your biggest influence will be your opportunity to model steadfast love, even if your stepchild does nothing to deserve it. In fact, it may count the most when your stepchild least deserves it. You could be the target of misplaced anger and sadness, and it's easy (and justified) to feel resentment. But God will undoubtedly use your undeserved love to shape your stepchild's life. Offering this kind of love will require you to receive from God what you are not receiving from your stepchild. But you trigger God's power when you choose to love, and you will feel your heart strengthened as you act on your love. This may sound mysterious, but 1 John 4:12 affirms that God fills us and shines through us when we express His love to others.

As stepparents, we sometimes manifest this love through our resilience. Your continued openness to your child will make a difference—even when it looks like there is no response. Your steadfast love may be used to change your child's trajectory. But even if it doesn't, God will use it to change you.

You show this kind of love by not letting your stepchildren's up-and-down behavior measure the love you offer them. This is no easy task, and the way your love is manifested will have to take different forms. Sometimes you will need to express your love a bit more distantly while your stepchildren sort out all that is going on inside them. Other times, God may draw you and your stepchild close together and use your love to heal something in him or her that someone else broke. Your willingness to love—even when it's not reciprocated—will be what God uses most in your stepchild's life.

If you start with the goal of love in mind, you will be more alert to opportunities to connect with your stepchild at each stage of your relationship. Focus on what you can do right now rather than what you wish was different, and you will find many ways to participate in your stepchild's life. By becoming an observer and a listener, you can discover points of connection that allow you to grow in your relationship and influence. Even with your parental limitations, you will be surprised at the opportunities that unfold before you when you commit to your call.

SHOWING UP

When I was a youth pastor, I had one piece of advice for new volunteers wanting to connect with kids in my youth ministry: Find out what a student is involved in and just show up. When students saw that they mattered enough for someone to come see them or support them, it accomplished something intangible. I watched life-changing relationships begin in my ministry when caring adults took the time to show up in students' lives. The same can be true of stepparenting.

You may think you have no choice but to show up, particularly when the child is living in your home and you can't really avoid it. However, showing up is more than coexisting—it's being intentional with your presence, especially as you begin your role. One of the primary challenges for stepparents is to avoid pushing a child toward an intimate parent-child relationship before the child is ready for it. Trying to impose closeness can actually work against you, and your presence without that pressure can ease you into a relationship that is natural and unforced. Simply being there intentionally can be a way to help your child to get to know you without feeling rushed toward intimacy. It allows your relationship to form at a comfortable pace and enables your child to lead on how close you become.

Researcher James Bray confirms this advice when he says the best way to forge a relationship with stepchildren is to begin by monitoring their activities. Depending on the child's age, this may simply be providing care when needed, or if the child is older, showing up for practices, performances, or games. You show your support for your stepchild by showing up and watching them even before you have established emotional closeness. It is a simple way to demonstrate your care in a nonthreatening way and build a bridge that will one day connect your hearts.[2]

The first day I took Jordan to school, I had my first opportunity to show up in his life the way James Bray suggested. Many of the parents were signing up to volunteer in the classroom, and though I briefly flashed on my "I'm just the stepparent" limitation, I suddenly realized what a great opportunity it could be. I saw some other moms helping out in Jordan's second-grade classroom and observed how proud and happy their kids were to have them there. (Every parent should consider volunteering in elementary school, because years later, kids don't want parents anywhere near their room.) I thought having a parent show up might feel good for Jordan and help establish his place in a brand-new environment. It was an opportunity for me to see him outside of our home, and I thought that might bring us closer together in a nonthreatening way.

The first day I arrived to volunteer, I was assigned to work with a boy in Jordan's class named Luke, and it was apparent he and Jordan were on different reading tracks. Jordan's previous school had taught only sight words, and when I listened to sentences rolling out of Luke's mouth while he read, I thought, *We're going to need some help.*

My next assignment was Ryan, who appeared to be a second-grade PhD candidate. Panic set in when I heard Ryan read through his entire book in five minutes, but the teacher assured me after class that Jordan would be fine. She said that kids at this age catch up fast, and an extra hour or two of reading after school would do it. By showing up to volunteer in Jordan's class, I was given a window into a need that I could meet. I would have missed this opportunity if I hadn't been there.

On the afternoon of our first reading session, we huddled together as he made his way through sentences at a pace you only know if you've listened to a new reader. It went something like this: "The…rr…ed…ff… ire…tru…ck…ro…lled…in…to…the…sta…tion…" When we got to the end of a sentence, I'd give a cheer. Being a person who rarely slows down, it was easy to see God had a purpose for me in those after-school moments. With more deep breaths and tongue biting than I care to admit, my time listening to Jordan read wasn't just for his growth—it was for me.

After a few weeks of working through words like a warrior, Jordan started powering through books and eventually caught up to all his classmates. Ryan went on to get straight A's and start a million-dollar business in high school, so he doesn't count. But the important thing was that something besides Jordan's success in reading transpired because of all those after-school moments. Our relationship grew in ways that never would have happened if it wasn't for the time and experience we had shared.

Two years later, Jordan entered a fourth-grade reading contest in which he had to read ten books in nine months—a goal only a few students accomplished. The teacher held a ceremony to give those students a "master's" degree, and I bawled as if our boy was receiving the real thing. Those after-school hours of reading all came flooding back as I reveled in his joy at his accomplishment. It was the story God began writing when I decided to look for opportunities to support Jordan and take the time to show up.

Those after-school memories stand out as some of the biggest bonding experiences I've had with Jordan. When I heard him read his first sentences, I felt like I witnessed a rite of passage that everyone else missed. As a stepparent, these bonding experiences are gifts, and I discovered that when you show up for the little things, sometimes that opens the door to bigger things. You may not be able to volunteer in your stepchild's classroom, but you can always find ways to show up to help. It may feel awkward at times, and you may experience feelings of rejection, but much of your job as a stepparent is to not let your insecurity stop you. Even if your stepchildren initially respond with indifference, you never know what showing up might eventually produce.

SHOWING UP WHEN IT'S HARD

When he arrived at his stepdaughter's volleyball game, he wasn't sure if he might ultimately regret it. But a force moved in him that day to show her he was there for her regardless of whether she ever wanted him in her life. For many years she had greeted him at her games with a hug, a smile, and "Thanks for coming, Dad." Now that her mom had divorced him, he was treated as if he were invisible. Still, he maintained his commitment to love her in spite of her response.

He found a seat in the upper corner of the bleachers and kept a low-key presence. Since she hadn't wanted anything to do with him, he didn't want his presence to be too obvious for fear it would distract her. He brought her half-brother with him, and at halftime he encouraged his young son to run down the bleachers to see her. He stayed where he was, not wanting to make her uncomfortable, but he watched with gladness for the joy her brother brought to her face. Though he left without a glance or a word from her, he would say he was glad he had done it. What he didn't know was that it was the first crack in the ice around her heart that would take two more years to thaw.

This story is my husband's story with his stepdaughter after her mother divorced him. As I mentioned in chapter 1, he had raised two stepchildren from her previous marriage, but they were now only related to him by choice. His stepson had stayed connected to him and even participated in our wedding, but Jere's relationship with his stepdaughter was strained by her anger over what happened. This broke Jere's heart because she had embraced him as her dad her whole life. Her own dad had long ago moved out of the country, and largely out of her life, and Jere had gladly stepped up to fill the hole. He took her on school camping trips, traveled with her to volleyball tournaments, and loved her as his own. But the divorce left her heartbroken, and because Jere was the parent who would no longer be related to her, she had stopped speaking to him. When Jere showed up at the game, it was right in the middle of the storm.

The story continued after that game, with many more weeks and months of putting pieces of love back together. During the first year of our marriage, I happened to be asked to speak at her college chapel, and because she stood in line after to meet me, I got to play a part. She and I had immediate rapport and started communicating, but when I offered that Jere and I could bring Jordan to meet her for coffee, the road of healing was slow and tenuous. In our first few meetings, she barely glanced in Jere's direction, so she and I and Jordan mostly conversed around him while he bravely sat still in his love. In time, the ice melted, and when she decided to move back to our town, she became a regular guest at meals with our patched-together family. It was a gift for me to be a part of the reconciliation story, but it was Jere's consistent love—and willingness to show up—that brought her back into our lives.

When you let go of expectations for your relationship with your stepchild, you leave room for God's surprise in how He shapes and forms it. Some roads in your relationship will seem to take you in an ominous direction, but you may discover they are included in the journey because they are part of the healing God wants to do. Keep your eyes on your own actions and responses, and your resilience and perseverance will allow God's love to keep chasing them.

Don't write the end of the story too soon; instead, pray for strength to wait things out, and never give up. You can't see what might be ahead, and your trust in what God is able to do can sustain you in your current circumstances. God is a master at weaving together a story you could never write, and the timeline is often longer than you imagine. Jere experienced that when he and his stepdaughter went on a date for her twenty-eighth birthday, and they were able to have an honest conversation that fully mended their hearts.

The stepparenting journey is long, with many hurtful chapters of not being recognized, loved, or acknowledged. Knowing you are participating in a much bigger story helps you find the impetus to draw on God's love and keep showing up. You may not immediately see results, but your consistency will allow your stepchild to experience a steadiness in your love for them. Your love will be a place they can always return to, and it will be the unshakeable influence you'll have on their lives.

FINDING BRIDGES
BETWEEN YOUR HEARTS

As Jere and I settled in the first row of the school auditorium to watch the sixth-grade musical, I'll admit my expectations were elementary sized. Our boy was playing Gaston in *Beauty and the Beast*, so that was all we needed to push our way to front-row seats. While we tried to find a comfortable way to sit in our folding chairs (does it even exist?), I thought back to all the performances that had led me to choose a theater arts major in college. The stage had always been my passion, and even though I took it in a different direction, when Jordan announced he got a lead in his sixth-grade musical, my heart leaped.

When he came out on stage and belted his first song, I had my first "That's my kid!" moment. Jordan's dad and I obnoxiously stuck our iPhones in the air taking videos, and when he finished his song, our heads were three times their original size. He was spectacular (every parent says that, but he really was), and my excitement was personal because of my love for the theater. When I watched him strut on stage, I felt as if this child somehow *got* something I had. Performing had always given me that juice, and it was clear by Jordan's enjoyment on stage that he, too, was drinking it. It was a connection between us around a passion I now could clearly see we both had.

As a stepparent, your path of connection to your stepchild is different from a biological parent's. Theirs evolves from inbred connections; yours comes from connections that you have to look for between you—connections that don't come from genes. Pay attention to what they are drawn to that interests you or that you are skilled at, and it can become your bridge of connection. A talent, an interest, a food preference…even the smallest thing can bring you together around something you both like. You'll be more apt to connect in a meaningful way if you have a genuine interest in what your stepchild is doing. My enthusiasm for Jordan's video games may lack a certain energy, but the excitement I feel watching him perform can't be faked.

Since Gaston, he's gone on to play a butcher, an animated clock, and Prince Charming. Because I don't have biology to claim, I can objectively say that he is one of the most talented kids I've ever seen. (Humor me.) He owns the stage with every part, and with the musical talents he inherited from his parents, I can't wait to watch his opportunities unfold. I ultimately used my stage experience to infuse my speaking career, and I know there are many ways this talent could enhance his life. I have helped him craft speeches, cheered him on rehearsing his plays, and watched his stage presence bloom while leading worship. I will be thrilled to see how his gift in performing manifests itself in his future life. When you are on the lookout for the things you share with your stepchildren, you will find a place to imprint them with your influence. You will also see more evidence of why God may have planned to have you in their lives.

Whether it's something in them you are there to encourage, or a hole God wants you to fill, you will discover God's design in placing you with your stepchildren. You will see not only how you are used in your stepchild's life but also how God uses your stepparenting to do something in you.

Even if you never see all that God does through you in your stepchild's life, your heart will grow bigger because of the way stepparenting stretches you. Your calling will give you peace that you are there for a reason, and as little or as big as that reason might be, you know you are playing some part in your stepchild's development. Your response is simply to open your heart and eyes for how that part is to be played.

A DEEPER NEED YOU MAY BE CALLED TO MEET

I remember sitting in the giant auditorium where my friend got married, watching her thirteen-year-old son stand between her and her groom as they approached the altar. It was clear her groom was getting a package deal, and as her new husband, he was visually declaring his commitment to the stepparent role. Knowing the background of the story, I was aware of the redemption unfolding before me. I also recognized the difficulty they were embarking on and breathed a grateful sigh about the challenging role he was willing to take.

My friend's first husband had several indiscretions marked by sexual abuse that had left her broken. The day she was thrust into a single-parent role, she barricaded her heart and decided never to marry again and settled into raising her three-week-old son. For eleven years, the two of them lived in a beautifully decorated trailer parked in the driveway between her parents' and sister's houses. With the help of her family and church, she heroically did her best to create a loving and stable home.

When Johnny exploded into her life, she did the same as with all her other prospects—she held him at bay and told him all she could ever offer was friendship. He took what she had to offer, and after three years of declaring by his presence that he was going nowhere, the broken pieces of her heart slowly healed. She saw the role model he had become to her son, and that deepened her affection for him. She was at the stage of needing to back away as a mother, and with the holes left from her ex-husband's indiscretion and abuse, her boy needed the example of a trustworthy man.

Johnny was a volunteer in her youth group, and he fell in love with my friend while watching her parent her son and run a ministry. He had never married, but if she would have him, he would gladly step into the stepfather role. For three long years it seemed like it would never happen as she stayed walled up against his overtures. But his persistence was the balm she needed to be able to grace him with her heart.

When Johnny decided to propose, he brought his future stepson in on planning it. To this day, that has stayed with my friend as one of the dearest of all the gifts Johnny brought to her life. He went to her boy's school and wrote a note to excuse him, and together they filled his house with flowers. They even set up a track with his old toy train to deliver the ring. When she walked in the house, she was overwhelmed; but when she saw who was behind it, she was speechless with gratitude. Since I opened this story seated in the grand auditorium of their wedding, you can guess what happened next.

After she and Johnny got back from their honeymoon, the three of them set up house together. After being single and childless, Johnny began his journey into marriage with one of the most daunting step-parent roles imaginable. There were many stressful moments when this dear couple was stretched by the circumstances surrounding their parenting. Figuring out boundaries between their boy and his biological dad, and what Johnny's part should be within that, brought them to counseling—and to their knees. Even with the beauty of their story, the difficulty of shared parenting put a strain on their marriage they couldn't have imagined.

But it also made them stronger as a couple, and the way their family has evolved is worth all the stretching they endured. That thirteen-year-old boy is now a college graduate. He had some rocky times, and his path to adulthood was long and windy. But there is no doubt in my friend's heart that Johnny's willingness to stand with her son in the years they had him in their home played a significant part in the man he's become.

When it comes to a stepparent's influence, there is no script to tell you how or what a child will get from you. In many cases, stepparents don't ever fully know what they brought to their stepchild's life. But if you love your stepchild with as much force (or softness) as God allows, you can rest assured you will play a part in influencing them. I know this because even with a stepmother three years older than me, her consistent love has had an influence on me. No matter how your step-children feel about you right now, hold firm in your position of loving them. That may be your legacy of influence, even if that is all God uses you to do.

A FINAL WORD ON INFLUENCE

Because of my years as a youth pastor, I've been aware for a long time of the power of influence. I've not only watched mentoring relationships shape students from difficult family situations, I've seen how people outside my biological family had an influence on me that led to monumental shifts in who I became. Biology may give us our traits and mannerisms, but the influence of adults who walk alongside us can shape our lives in ways that transform us. Seeing your stepparenting as an opportunity to have this kind of impact heightens the way you occupy this role.

There will be times when you won't think you matter, when you are put off by your stepchild's indifference or feel overwhelmed by the challenge before you. Remember that this time of raising your stepchildren is temporary, and in a certain amount of years, it will just be you and your spouse. For the time you've been given, my hope is that you will recognize the weight of the opportunity in front of you. Because you are there, God believes you have what it takes to fulfill your call.

The Inside Job of Stepparenting

There's nothing like the difficulty of stepparenting to uncover some things you may not want to see about yourself. On the other hand, there is nothing like the difficulty of stepparenting to call out strength that you never thought you could achieve. You carry a label with a stereotype you'd rather not have, and on your wedding day, you were presented with a child to parent who isn't yours. From there, you moved into a family that may include members who don't want you there.

Stepparenting can be a breeding ground for insecurity, fear, and jealousy. It can also be an opportunity to see some of the ways you might be contributing to these feelings—which you have the power to heal and change. You probably know this, but some of your triggers and emotions were present in you before you began your marriage. The stress of stepparenting can bring things to the surface that you brought in from a previous relationship, or even from the family where you were raised. No one enters marriage in a vacuum, but stepparenting allows you to see your "stuff" much quicker. The pressure involved in finding your place in a stepfamily can call up feelings inside you that first marriages don't always bring up. You may not be able to change the dynamics of what is going on around you, but you can let them move you to explore what may be going on inside you. In that respect, the difficulty of stepparenting can sometimes turn out to be a gift.

It might be easy for your stepparenting situation to make you feel powerless, but because you are in it, *you* are part of what happens to you. I want to encourage you in this chapter to see what you bring into your circumstances that you have a chance to change. It's a bit of a scary journey because it requires you to be honest with what is going on inside of you. It's easier to fault others for what we feel (and there may be legitimate reasons to do that), but when we do that, we give away all the power in our stepparent role. There is no doubt that as a stepparent, you will face things that are unfair, unjustified, and painful. But self-awareness may help shine a light into the part your feelings play in the way you take things in. If you discover what is behind your feelings and responses, you can monitor some of the impact that your stepchildren, spouse, and biological counterpart will have on you. You will also prevent any fear or insecurity that you may have brought into your marriage from adding to the already difficult circumstances you face. Sometimes, this process of confronting your "stuff" begins before the marriage even takes place.

THE GHOST OF
RELATIONSHIPS PAST

Sipping my salted caramel mocha, I was in a moment of perfect bliss...until a wave of fear sent chills up and down my body. This beautiful man was sitting before me, but I was scared to death at what was happening to my heart. We had limited ourselves to meeting weekly at Starbucks so we could move slow, but things were happening inside me that weren't minding my blueprint. I was terrified to let my heart start down this road because of where it had previously led. Five years earlier, I had a whirlwind romance with a Marine that had resulted in a year-long engagement. Our wedding was postponed by his sudden deployment; and after two showers, a purchased wedding dress, and furniture picked out for our home, I found myself standing at Camp Pendleton waving goodbye to the bus as he left. In the time he was gone, his ex-wife apparently communicated second thoughts about divorcing him. When he came home nine months later, our wedding was called off because he remarried her instead.

Let me pause here and say that as a Christian, I truly believe that this is a great story of reconciliation. My fiancé's ex had left the marriage years earlier, and our engagement and his deployment caused her to see what she had given up—so she went to work to win him back. In many ways it was a God story, and though I didn't love my part in it, I was glad for their kids that they were able to find a way to move forward. However, my heart barely survived, and this experience left me extremely tender at the prospect of playing this role again.

The only script I knew was that if Jere and I fell in love and got engaged, his ex-wife might come back to him. But deep inside, I knew if I never worked through my fear of being left again, this new relationship could never work out. So you can understand my terror as my heart started pounding in our little Starbucks. Only my courage to risk loss again could move me through the fear I faced.

Jere had already gone to his ex-wife twice to see if there was any chance for reconciliation. She had moved into another relationship and had no interest, but because of the trauma of my previous situation, there was no way of calming my fears. However, I didn't want my previous experience to sabotage what Jere and I could have if I took the risk to move forward. Looking back, it was the courage to face that fear that strengthened my heart for the challenges that lay ahead.

Fear begins to heal when you stop avoiding it and turn to face it. Ironically, it is in the facing of it that healing is found. Somehow when you are willing to not run away, the fear is minimized. It is not what happens afterward that heals you; it's the act of moving forward in the storm. You may not change the storm, but when you change who you are in it, the storm doesn't affect you in the same way. This same principle applies with the difficult circumstances you will encounter throughout your stepparenting that will require your inner strength.

Ron Deal uses the term "ghosts" to talk about some of the fears from the past that people bring into their marriages and stepfamilies.[1] Ghosts are memories from a previous relationship or your family of origin, and when they come up to haunt you, they can influence (and potentially sabotage) what is in front of you right now. Your response to what is happening now is colored by what happened in the past. You react with the emotion left unhealed by your past experience, and this may cause you to see your current situation as being worse than it actually is. Even sadder, your ghost may cause you to write an ending to your new story before the story has a chance to unfold. My ghost was abandonment, and the prospect of moving forward after my broken engagement forced me to confront my fear. The opportunity to step forward and risk the same thing happening again offered me a strength I would gain no matter what the future entailed. That is true of all ghosts—the moment you turn and face them, they lose their power to intimidate you. In that respect you can be thankful for past insecurities and fears that are reignited in your marriage and stepparenting, because facing those ghosts in your present circumstances gives you an opportunity to make them disappear.

The Smart Stepfamily mentions several ghosts that are common in second marriages.[2] It could be an issue of jealousy, rejection, mistrust, or hidden behaviors you experienced in a previous relationship—and these fears may trigger you to interpret your spouse's behavior through your ghost instead of what is actually there. When you are marrying into a stepfamily, your insecurities become compounded by the presence of an ex-spouse and stepchildren. That is why it is important to face any fear you may be bringing into your marriage—so it doesn't add to the difficulty of relationships *around* your marriage that you need to negotiate for your marriage and family to succeed.

One difficulty with ghosts is that if you continue responding out of fear of them, you sometimes create a self-fulfilling prophecy. If I had let my fear stop me from moving forward with Jere, I would have lost the relationship—and exactly what I feared would have taken place. The same is true of any of the ghosts you may bring into your marriage or stepparenting. If you have a fear of abandonment, you might pull away or hover too close, which will inevitably create distance. If you feel insecure about your spouse's relationship with his children, you might require attention taken from the kids that will put your relationship with your spouse in an awkward place. These feelings need to be acknowledged, but when we overact out of our fears, the very thing we fear can sometimes end up taking place.

There is a story in the Old Testament book of Numbers that illustrates this principle. The Israelites were about to receive the very thing they wanted. God had led them to the edge of the promised land and told them He wanted to deliver it to them, but they had to go in and conquer what was there. Twelve of them were sent in to scout the land so they could develop a strategy to go in and take it. They found everything just as God said it would be, but when they came back to report about it, fear colored what they saw. The more they fed their fear, the bigger their fear grew, until they worked everyone up into a frenzy. Ultimately the group decided they would rather go back to the land of slavery than move forward into the land of freedom. God offered them an opportunity to conquer their fears with His help, but they were too focused on those fears to see past them. In the end, the very thing they were afraid of happened—not because they lost a battle, but because they never went in to fight (see Numbers 13–14).

God gives us situations to face our fears and beat them, and being a part of a stepfamily can be a great opportunity for this to happen. Whether you've brought something in from a previous relationship or from your family of origin, God may use a similar issue in your marriage and stepparenting to heal you. It's important to acknowledge your feelings and even share them so your spouse can be sensitive to avoid triggering them. But some of your fears will arise even with your spouse's sensitivity, and this will be an opportunity for you to develop the strength to face other stepparenting storms. As the story in Numbers 13 illustrates, the only way to get rid of a fear is to face it. When you do that, your fear diminishes and you are positioned to courageously face the challenges ahead.

Is what you are feeling legitimate for what you are experiencing right now, or is it tied to an experience from the past? And how can you even tell? Conquering your ghosts doesn't mean ignoring your feelings; it means understanding where your feelings come from and whether they are appropriate for the situation you now face. There might be something about your current situation that has triggered something bigger from your past, so it's more about discerning the level of your feelings and their source.

Author Wednesday Martin talks about a time when her stepdaughters' possessiveness for their father enraged her, and she began exploring where her anger came from. Their feelings of entitlement—"Daddy is ours, and we don't want to share him"—would have frustrated any stepparent, but her feelings of rage tapped into something bigger. A therapist helped her see that her stepdaughters had a closeness with her husband that she didn't have with her own father. When her therapist helped her to see the connection, she could see her situation and responses more clearly and adjust what didn't belong.[3]

When you connect the dots between your reactions and your fears, you may be able to see where you are interpreting some behavior to a greater degree than the behavior merits. If you suspect you might be overreacting, get an opinion from someone you trust about a situation you currently face. That outside support will help you determine whether you are responding appropriately or letting your fear hijack your response.

Healing your ghosts will take time, and you may need help to do it.

The important thing is to not allow your ghost to color your current circumstances to the point that your response creates something that isn't there. There will inevitably be complications in a second marriage because of all the relationships around your marriage that you and your spouse need the maturity to negotiate. Your self-awareness will help you discern what you need to look at in yourself and when you need to address a legitimate issue. Don't be like the spies from the story who went into the land looking for fear and found it. This is your opportunity to "take the land" of your marriage and stepfamily—and you don't want ghosts from the past to add to the challenges in front of you right now. Those challenges will require enough work on their own.

REASONABLE AND UNREASONABLE EXPECTATIONS

The first time I took Jordan to the park, we had an incredible time bonding together. We held hands on the slides, he yelled out for me to watch him on the jungle gym, and we took selfies on the park bench. I took him across the path to see the turtles in the pond, and he spent hours gazing at them. He stayed glued to my side, and it turned out to be the perfect day for us to bond. On the way home, he looked over at me in the car and said, "I'm so glad you're my second mommy."

Then my stepparenting dream ended, and I woke up.

What *actually* happened the first time I took him to the park was that he ran off into the play structure and never looked back until I went in to get him. He played with other kids while I sat alone with my iPhone camera, documenting his fun from afar. I took him to see the turtles—for about ten minutes—and we got one picture with an awkward half smile that revealed his enthusiasm in my taking it. But we made it to the park, and he seemed to have fun, and I counted it a win in my stepparenting book.

Reeling back expectations is one of the inside jobs we have as stepparents. One of the stepparents on my survey said it well when she wrote, "Keep your expectations low and your hopes high"—but this can be a delicate dance. Emily Visher, founder of the Stepfamily Association of America, says of all the things you bring into your stepfamily, "unrealistic expectations are the biggest risk."[4] They not only set you up for disappointment but also cause you to define something as a failure that could actually be a success. My so-so park trip revealed a minor (and, okay, slightly exaggerated) example of some of the unrealistic expectations we might have coming into our stepfamily. We might not even realize we have expectations. Visher names a few that may be lurking in your subconscious, and they will vary according to your personal situation going in. Perhaps one of these scenarios will resonate with you.

If you go into stepparenting with kids from both sides, you may think your kids will be excited to have new brothers or sisters. You picture something like *The Brady Bunch* (if you watch reruns), and when you encounter tension and conflict, you may feel your family is a fail. The truth is, your family will need a period of adjustment even if it grows to become the epitome of stepfamily success. The myth that a blended family should develop as a normal family can lead to frustration and disappointment before your stepfamily has a chance to evolve. Remember the Crock-Pot mentality (from chapter 2), and try to look at your evolving family as an adventure—like taking a trip to a place you've never been before. Prepare yourself inwardly for challenges, expect some problems and setbacks, and learn to celebrate every little bit of success. God is there to fill in the gaps of your imperfections. In fact, His power shines the brightest in our weakness.

If your stepkids aren't going to be living with you, you may go into your marriage thinking that they will have little to no impact on your spouse or new family. Then, when summer or visitation time hits and the kids *are* with you, you might be unprepared for the disruption and strain that ensues. Remember that you married a person with children, and even if the children are grown up or don't live with you, your spouse's former family will bring inevitable adjustments and sacrifices. Lean into those times and let them teach you. The moments that require our flexibility and patience are the moments God uses most powerfully to show us things about ourselves. You may be surprised what your adult stepchildren can bring to your life.

If you are single with no children of your own when you come into your stepfamily, you might picture something like *The Sound of Music*. There may be a little adjustment, but in time you will sing your way into your stepchildren's hearts. The problem is, even if you love your children perfectly (which you won't), they will always have a biological mommy or daddy. This is true even if that mommy or daddy is deceased. If your relationship evolves to become the best it could possibly be, you will still discover the dynamics between you and your stepchild will be impacted by the biological parent. Ironically, the more you love your stepchild, the more you will have to work through feelings of jealousy and insecurity of being the second mom (or dad). This process can be especially difficult when stepchildren are your only children, but if you continue to be aware that your children have two moms or dads, you will be better prepared for the inevitable feelings. Don't expect that those feelings will necessarily get easier with time.

Visher adds that one of the most brutal expectations stepparents hold is that everyone in the stepfamily will eventually love each other. She offers this alternative: "Go for reasonable. Go for content. Go for 'we're working on it.'" And I would add, remember that the only love you can control is yours. As someone who likes to be liked, I discovered in my own stepparenting journey that the more "being liked" was my goal, the less likely it was to happen. Trying for a certain response or outcome can also lead to resentment when your goal isn't met. The relationships in your stepfamily will require freedom, and the best way to help those relationships form naturally is to let go of how you think it will happen. Love is most successful (and often most responded to) when it comes with no strings attached.

A final expectation many of us deal with is that once we have established a solid relationship with our stepchild, we won't have any more conflict or adversity. The truth is, like all familes, you will go through many different seasons with your stepchild, and they may bring new challenges for you to face. Because I worked with teenagers for so long, I had an expectation that once Jordan hit adolescence, he would *really* love me. I believed that this was the stage when I'd feel most confident in my parenting because I already knew how to relate to teenagers so well.

The truth is, his teenage years have been my most difficult and have required me to do some inside work on my self-esteem and my confidence in stepparenting. I laugh when I think back to my years as a youth pastor, meeting with parents in my office as I patronizingly put my arm around them and said, "Things are going to be just fine." More than once I have met with Jordan's youth pastor and cried on his shoulder about my own insecurities. His perspective and support has been incredibly valuable, just as mine once was to the parents of kids in my group.

This is a stage where Jordan is closer to Jere, and he is also talking more to his biological mom, so his independence and occasional indifference to me has required me to once again revisit my stepparent expectations. Sometimes your stepchild's healthy development will mean a loss or an adjustment in what you receive back. Remembering that truth helps you recover your mission for what you are called to do.

The inside job of adjusting your expectations is an ongoing process. It's not a "one and done" thing, because your expectations shift and change with time. You will need to monitor them as long as you live. Tempering your expectations also helps you appreciate things as wins and learn to celebrate small victories (feel free to borrow my park story). Share your stories with other stepparents so you can pat each other on the back. The more secure you can be with who you are— regardless of your stepchild's response—the more peace you'll have in your stepparenting. Find ways to fill your own heart with affirmation, and don't let your expectation of a certain response shape your definition of success.

JEALOUSY, RESENTMENT, ENVY, AND OTHER EMOTIONS WE DENY

I am pretty sure no one writes "prone to jealousy" on their bio. Instead, it's a feeling that unhappily takes us by surprise. Recently when I walked by Jordan's closed bedroom door, I heard a peel of laughter that was currently absent in my relationship with him. From the time he had hit adolescence, the most common sound emanating from his mouth toward me was a sigh of disgust. I assumed it was one of his friends, and when I asked him later who it was, he said he was talking to his mom from Australia. The pit in my stomach came so fast, I had no time to interrupt it with my "I shouldn't feel that way" guilt.

Perhaps the least attractive character quality we confront in ourselves as stepparents is our inevitable feeling of jealousy. Our response to that feeling is often disappointment or disgust because we feel like stereotypical fairy-tale villains. As stepmothers, any feelings of jealousy may conjure up pictures from "Snow White" or "Cinderella." The image of a chore-demanding, apple-carrying witch causes us to push down and bury legitimate feelings, hoping we can act them away. However, a more helpful and healing response is to dive into the feeling, uncover the fear behind the jealousy, and address that fear.

Fairy-tale stepmothers often betray the envy that lurks behind the jealousy. Melanie Klein says that "envy is the malicious, angry, destructive feelings we have when we believe someone else possesses a quality which we prize yet feel we lack."[5] This is abusively displayed in the behavior of Snow White's and Cinderella's stepmothers, but it can sometimes surface within us. We want to avoid acting like these fairy-tale stepmothers, who treated their stepdaughters with wickedness and contempt.

Stepdads are given a more benign portrayal of jealousy in the 2015 film *Daddy's Home*, in which two dads (one step, one biological) compete for their children's attention. These dads are able to reach a humorous and happy resolution—a stark contrast to the stereotype of stepmothers that second moms must endure. We have to realize that all these depictions—no matter how exaggerated—represent honest feelings. We need to acknowledge those feelings even as we temper the actions we take in response to them. As a stepmother, I recommend avoiding poisonous apples and mirrors on walls.

To describe the emotions we stepparents tend to experience, researcher Elizabeth Church puts them in the context of a three-way or triangular relationship. One person in the triangle is jealous of a loved one's relationship with another person—so as a stepparent, your jealousy may stem from your spouse's relationship with his child or his relationship with his ex. It may take shape in feeling competition with your stepchildren for your spouse's love, or feeling jealous of your child's biological parent (like I did when I walked by Jordan's bedroom door). Elizabeth Church gives this helpful counsel: "Our susceptibility to jealousy is affected by the degree of security we feel."[6] As stepparents, this is the place we can explore.

In our quest for healthy stepparenting, we must continue learning how to reestablish our inner security. Going back to my scene at Jordan's door, I simply needed to acknowledge my embarrassing (yet understandable) feelings to myself and then reaffirm my call. As the stepparent, my job will always include affirming Jordan's relationship with his biological mom. The more I encourage and support that relationship, the better and closer my relationship with Jordan will be. Competition and jealousy never evoke love; they only complicate relationships and create distance. Keep the end goal of your stepparent relationship in sight—that will help you to prevent your feelings from interrupting your call.

So what (if anything) can be done to subdue your jealous feelings? Your spouse can be extremely helpful in your triangular relationships because he or she is included in two out of three. Consider reading the following sentences aloud to your partner so they can hear these thoughts from someone other than you: Stepparents can feel like a disregarded third wheel when their feelings are unintentionally overlooked. Your spouse may not be focused on your feelings when the children are with you, but your spouse's awareness of your feelings can cause him to notice when he and his children unintentionally exclude you.

When a new stepfamily is first coming together, the children naturally crave closeness with their biological parent apart from you. It's important for you as a stepparent to understand and support that, but the biological parent needs to be aware that he or she has more power to start including you than you do. Finding ways to ease the children in to being comfortable with both of you—rather than seeing you as competition or a threat—helps to establish and strengthen your bond.

As Elizabeth Church points out, jealousy (especially for stepmothers) generally masks one of three things: powerlessness, resentment, or a feeling of being taken for granted.[7] Sometimes a stepparent's love for a child is never reciprocated, and sometimes your relationship evolves to be incredibly rewarding, but there is no guarantee of what you will get in return for your love. To some extent, that is true for every relationship, but the stepparent-stepchild relationship can be one of the most one-sided. If we are unable to change our stepchildren's behavior, we might do better by adjusting our own.[8] Setting boundaries around what you can and cannot do is better than doing something with an expectation of a response that may not come.

Only you can determine how freely you can give of yourself without a subtle (and often unrecognized) need to get something back from your stepchild. In my relationship with Jordan, I have found that I need to check and recheck this expectation at every turn. You are not called to be abused and taken for granted by your stepchild, but you are called to love selflessly. In order to do that in a healthy way and to avoid developing resentment, you may have to set some boundaries. Your stepchildren are likely to respect you more if you don't allow them to step all over you (no pun intended). Taking care of yourself is one of your biggest jobs as a stepparent, and only you can determine what that will look like in your role.

Perhaps the last word in this chapter should be given to a stepparent who gave this piece of advice on my survey: "Always be true to yourself." The first time I read it I thought it sounded selfish, but it may be the best way stepparents can love freely and selflessly. If your actions require a validating response from your child or spouse, you are probably (inadvertently) creating a breeding ground for resentment. You may even be unintentionally setting up your family to fail. Stepfamily relationships require you to be mature enough to pay attention to what is going on inside of you. You need to be honest with yourself about what you can offer without expectation of what you will get back.

In my own experience, giving love unconditionally is possible only with a reservoir of God's love to draw from. Even then, because of my human nature, it's surprising how a pocket of resentment can build up. Stepparenting requires an ongoing personal inventory of our expectations, which can be hidden even to ourselves behind our actions and responses. With a gut check, you will be able to set boundaries when you need to, get support when you feel weak, and be free to give yourself to your role.

6

When Unfair Is Okay

When I was getting a master's degree at Fuller Seminary, my ethics professor left such a vivid impression on me that I can still picture him. His name was Lewis Smedes, and he would whisk into class like Jimmy Stewart, with white hair tumbling down his forehead and childlike curiosity on his eighty-year-old face. He would begin every class with a question—usually about what was right or wrong in some complex issue. If you raised your hand to comment, he would savor your words as if they were the most important thoughts in the world at that moment. After a pause, he would cock his head and smile and counter with another question. Nothing was ever fully resolved, but a great deal of learning occurred.

In the end I was left with an appreciation of the complexity of right and wrong. Any stance on any issue must take so many other viewpoints into consideration! But there was one response that created a variable in all conclusions, and when this powerful posture entered the equation, it turned dead ends into new beginnings. Dr. Smedes eventually devoted a book to this transforming truth, and the title of his bestselling book alone is powerful enough to make sense of this chapter.

In *Forgive and Forget,* Dr. Smedes summed up the posture of forgiveness with these words: "Our sense of fairness tells us people should pay for the wrong they do. But forgiving is love's power to break nature's rules."[1]

With these words, I begin this chapter with a disclaimer. Without some kind of faith in God, much of what is in this chapter could be tough to swallow and may make no sense. However, in a book called *Grace-Filled Stepparenting,* this chapter may be the most important one in the book. Assuming you have already made your way through my faith bias at this point, you are either on the same page or adept at bypassing. You may need to bypass this chapter altogether unless you are open to the miracles that can happen inside our hearts. As chapter 5 made clear, a stepparent's job can feel thankless and could lead to deep resentment. But another response is available to us, and while it may feel incongruous to circumstances that are clearly unfair, it is the only one capable of setting us free. I invite you to go back and breathe in Dr. Smedes's words in the preceding paragraph one more time as we begin a stepparent's journey toward forgiveness and grace.

THINGS THAT ARE UNFAIR

When you begin compiling a list of all that is unfair about stepparenting, you may be at your desk several days. The truth is, such lists rarely exist—except the secret ones in our hearts. We know the list is there when something triggers our blowup, and we realize a pile of things underneath it became kindle without us even knowing it. So in order to keep the pile from growing, we need to recognize each unfair experience so we can remove it from our hearts. The unique thing about stepparenting is that people rarely realize or acknowledge the things they do that hurt us. Because everyone in a stepfamily has their own angle of unfairness, you must find a way to deal with your own.

Blanket forgiveness over everything that is unfair isn't possible, because forgiveness doesn't happen generally. We have to let go of each act of unfairness, or it gets buried and surfaces at an unexpected time. My beloved professor said it this way: "Ordinary people forgive best if they go at it in bits and pieces, and for specific acts. They bog down when they try to forgive in the grand manner, because wholesale forgiveness is almost always fake."[2] Wholesale forgiveness isn't a good strategy, especially when it comes to stepparenting. The web of relationships and feelings is too big, and one buried feeling of bitterness can tie itself to future decisions and conversations without you even knowing it's there. As Dr. Smedes suggests, it's best to forgive in bits and pieces and for specific acts that have hurt or angered you. Otherwise your bitterness can impact your future interactions and keep you from having a graceful response. Romans 12:18 says, "If it is possible, *as far as it depends on you*, live at peace with everyone." Peace at large may not be possible in your stepfamily, but forgiveness allows you to experience freedom from your need for retribution and gives you more peace in your heart.

Forgiveness comes slowly and clumsily, and we are likely to find ourselves doing it mostly or partially. I think I've let something go, but then I talk to a friend about it a week later so *they* will express what I obviously still feel. Somehow, holding on to unfairness gives us a false sense of control over what happened to us. We may feel we have such little control that we are tempted to use our anger or resentment as the one power we have. But the anger we hold on to can be the very thing our freedom demands we release. Otherwise our resentment ends up silently and often undetectably controlling us.

Philip Yancey says, "Ungrace does its work quietly and lethally, like a poisonous, undetectable gas."[3] This gas easily seeps into stepparenting, where ungrace is fueled by self-justification to further its poisonous effect. As stepparents, we can fill books over what we endure—and there may be some therapeutic merit in rehashing those things. However, if we don't eventually let go of them, we alone are left with the poison Yancey talks about, especially when the person who hurt us doesn't know or care. Forgiveness is not just a gift you give to others, it's the only way to extricate yourself from the bitterness that infects your peace and happiness. Forgiving someone who doesn't deserve it may seem unfair, but the one who suffers most by continuing to fight the battle of fairness is you. If you wait to extend forgiveness until a person apologizes, you become a hostage to the person who wronged you. Battles of fairness can create family pain for you, your stepchildren, and your marriage. Stepfamily feuds may go on endlessly because neither side owns what they've done to create anger and pain. Pains given and pains suffered never balance, because the pain someone inflicts on *you* always feels worse. The only way out of the cycle of revenge and retribution is for someone to be strong enough to wave the white flag of forgiveness. And while it may appear to be the weaker stance, it has the power to redirect the entire family's course.

The actual act of forgiveness requires discernment. Sometimes, telling the person how you feel in order to resolve a conflict is entirely appropriate. But there will be other times when silent forgiveness is the best course, and that leaves you alone with God to do the work of grace. Grace is hardest when someone doesn't know or care about what they've done to you and you feel as if you have every reason to withhold it. But even if the person never acknowledges what they've done (and you never tell them), the important thing to remember about extending grace is what it does for *you*.

Dr. Smedes says that when you replace fairness with forgiveness, you cut a malignant tumor out of your life and future. *Your* marriage, *your* relationships, and *your* heart will suffer if you hold on to bitterness and unfairness—even if they are completely justified—because those things take up residence inside your heart. That's the mystery of forgiveness. You think it's a gift you give someone who doesn't deserve it, but the truth is, it turns around and becomes a gift you give to *you*. When you release a wrongdoer from the wrong, you heal the pain of all the reruns of unfairness that reside in your heart and memory. In

Dr. Smedes's most quoted words, "You set a prisoner free, and discover that the real prisoner was yourself."[4]

So let's begin the work.

STEPFAMILY RELATIONSHIPS WHERE UNFAIRNESS OCCURS

Most of us would rather not acknowledge the unattractive feelings that lurk inside us. Personally, I would rather be seen as a martyr, so when I get angry about money issues, schedules, or unreasonable expectations in stepparenting, I usually end up telling a friend about it and adding, "But it's really okay." The problem is, it's really *not* okay, or I wouldn't be talking about it.

Rather than engaging in conversations with others to get them to react the way I feel, I need to take responsibility for my hurt or anger to let grace begin its work. Forgiveness can't happen if we deny that there is anything to forgive. This step is an important part of the process because you can't let go of what you don't admit you have. We have to see our need for grace in order to seek God to supply it. Coming to terms with the hurt or anger we feel helps us realize our own need for help. Whether you actually acknowledge your pain or anger to the person who hurt you depends on the relationship and the situation where unfairness occurred.

What doesn't work with grace is to approach the person who hurt or angered you and say "I forgive you." If the person hasn't recognized what they've done, saying "I forgive you" is merely telling them they should feel bad. In some relationships, having a conversation to confront the wrongdoing may be entirely appropriate. However, when it comes to the complex relationships in stepfamilies, the action you perceive to be unfair may feel completely justified to the person on the other side. That is why in stepfamily relationships, we often need to extend grace silently. This is the trickiest kind of grace because all the work is done inside you.

Every stepparent has an unfair story, and I've heard and read many of them. I thought about including my unfair stories, but every time I read those stories from others, I end up joining their resentment, and that seems unhelpful in a chapter about grace. What seems better is to identify some of the circumstances and relationships in stepfamilies where unfairness can be felt, and let you fill in the blanks of your own situation. You have your own stories of unfairness, and that is where you should focus as you consider the power of grace.

One final note to consider when letting go of unfairness is that if you have a relationship with God, you are equipped with an arsenal. More than once, the Bible refers to the undeserved grace we receive from God as a well for us to draw from when we have to extend that same kind of grace. Paul acknowledges this power in his own life in Ephesians 3:2, and in Romans 5:2 he says we *all* have access to it. God's grace is where you run when you have no reason to forgive, nowhere to put your unfairness, and no reserve of grace left on your own. God begins where you end—that's the mystery you experience when you extend undeserved grace.

Unfairness can occur in three main relationships: between you and your biological parent counterpart, between you and your stepchild, and between you and your spouse.

Often the biggest hotbed of potential emotion is between you and your biological parent counterpart because of emotions that were already present when you entered the scene. Unless you were the reason for your spouse's divorce, these feelings aren't personal to you, but they can impact your relationship. Add to that the possessiveness and feelings of jealousy that can easily crop up between you in your parenting, and you see how fragile this relationship can be. The myriad of feelings—largely unspoken—can impact some actions and responses between you that you will need to confront or absorb.

If your stepchildren are under eighteen, you and your biological parent counterpart will share custody, money division, responsibilities, and schedules. Many of the decisions for how these are executed will not be made by you, but they will greatly impact your life. If something feels unfair, you may be able to talk to your spouse, but you may not have any control over the way things are implemented. Ultimately you will decide how much you will let the unfairness you feel impact your heart. People who are co-parenting often have different perspectives of fairness, so this can make discussions complicated. "Fairness battles" can rage on and on without resolve, and the ones you choose to fight can leave scars that impact your stepfamily for years to come. Looking past what feels unfair to the damage the battle might create may help you make a decision to hold your tongue and opt for grace.

Keeping the big picture in mind while you are navigating your relationship with your biological parent counterpart makes you not feel like a victim of unfairness. Everyone wins in your stepfamily if you can find your way to peace. When you reflect on the grace that has been extended to you from a God who overlooks your unattractive behavior, it may help you decide to let go of some of your battles. Our own faults help us look at others more gently and ease our demand for justice in order to move ahead.

Sometimes you need to lose a battle of fairness in order to win a war in your stepfamily. The health of your marriage and stepchildren is far more important than making sure every co-parenting decision is fair, especially since many of those decisions will eventually fade away. Your silence may be building toward a better future, both relationally and spiritually. Stepchildren grow up and move away, and you are left with the relationships you cultivated while they were in your care. A lost battle of fairness may end up being a victory for peace in your family. It may also end up being a gift because God will use it to grow your soul.

The second relationship where unfairness occurs is between you and your stepchild—usually in the form of your stepchild's lack of appreciation or indifference to the sacrifices you make. What you experience when this happens falls under what Lewis Smedes calls "slights." You may not get the response or respect you deserve from your child, but this kind of unfairness is more passive in its blow. Slights are more common between older stepchildren and stepparents—especially at first, when the relationship is new and unfamiliar. Their behavior can range from ignoring you to saying (or showing) they don't like something you did. Slights hurt more when they stockpile, and they can bruise your self-esteem when they are ongoing. Most of the time your best response is to avoid taking slights personally or ignoring them, which is a different form of grace.

Understanding what may be behind your stepchild's behavior helps you draw from God's grace to cover it. Their actions often have to do with loyalty toward a biological parent or lingering hurt from their parents' divorce, which causes them to subconsciously push you away. When their hurtful behavior becomes more frequent or edges toward rudeness or cruelty, you or your spouse may need to speak up or set some boundaries. I join other stepfamily experts in recommending that this conversation is initiated by your spouse, who, as the biological parent, has the loudest voice. As time passes and you become more established as a part of the family, your voice in your stepchild's life will increase.

Ultimately, your resilience toward your stepchildren's behavior will win their respect and love as their understanding matures. You may walk a fine line between being resilient and being a doormat, and you will have to make that call. Sometimes the slights you experience (particularly in your child's teen years) don't have as much to do with stepparenting as they do with parenting in general. All parents are slighted by their kids during the teen years, and if you have part- or full-time custody, you get to be part of that club. You and your spouse need to discern whether your stepchild's behavior calls for their accountability or your resilience. And if it becomes clear that you need to sluff off their behavior, my recommendation is that you tell a friend all you have done for your stepchild without being appreciated, and let your friend give you the award ceremony you deserve.

Grace is essential for children of any kind, and it's an abundant need with stepchildren. You are the parent they acquired, so their love is, unfortunately, optional—and you may never get the appreciation you deserve. The next chapter will show you how to lower the bar and savor whatever affirmation you get from them. But you will need to draw from your well of God's grace for the underappreciation you will undoubtedly absorb in the role God has given you. It is a role God understands well.

The third relationship where unfairness can occur in stepparenting is between you and your spouse. This is hopefully the least frequent and least volatile, but it can happen when you don't talk about your expectations. Tensions flare up when your spouse hands you responsibilities you didn't expect. Of the three relationships, this one should allow you to express your feelings directly in order to solve the tension. If you aren't able to communicate your honest feelings to your spouse, you may need to solicit help from a counselor for your marriage to survive. Uncommunicated resentment can drive a wedge into a marriage and silently tear a couple apart.

Grace is not just needed for the relationships around your marriage—grace is needed within your marriage. You and your spouse face many pressures from the relationships around your marriage, so you may project feelings onto each other because they can't be communicated where they belong. You might also have to pick up the slack when your spouse's work schedule positions you as your stepchildren's primary caregiver. If your parenting responsibility is greater than you thought it would be, and you have a fragile relationship with your stepchildren, the pressure of these circumstances may cause your resentment to build. Keeping your communication open and your grace tank filled will help your marriage survive these tenuous times.

In all three of these stepfamily relationships, you will occasionally need to choose between fairness and forgiveness. Fairness is often a matter of perspective, so someone has to rescind their claim to fairness in order to stop the war. Silent forgiveness may feel like a weak response, especially when the person on the other side never acknowledges the pain or anger they've caused you. But fairness battles end up being unfair to you because they rob you of the energy you need to devote to other lifegiving relationships—especially since these battles may never be resolved. Only the extension of grace unlocks a future where the pursuit of fairness doesn't hold you under its grip.

In Dr. Smedes's words, "Forgiveness has creative power to move us away from a moment of pain, to unshackle us from our endless chain of reactions, and to create a new situation in which both the wrong-doer and the wronged can begin a new way."[5] Even if the one who has wronged you never knows it, your forgiveness releases *you* to have a new start. What you decide to do with your unfairness may ultimately have the last word in what happens in your stepfamily. Stepfamilies either buckle under resentment or move forward to peaceful and enriching relationships powered by grace.

While letting go of fairness may feel weak, you will win by staying open in your relationships. Fairness keeps people locked up and separated, whereas forgiveness builds bridges between imperfect people and allows broken families to heal. You may have to let go of what you feel you deserve or the kind of relationship you wish you had, but you will end up witnessing what grace can put together. When you keep fighting the battle of fairness, the person you end up being most unfair to is you.

A STORY OF FAIRNESS BRINGING LOSS

All his life, he did everything by the book to win the praise of his father. His younger brother, on the other hand, did everything he could to screw things up. He watched his brother run roughshod over his father's generosity, ultimately asking him for the unthinkable. His little brother had the gall to tell his father he wanted his inheritance early—he didn't want to wait for him to die to receive what would be his. He might as well have wished his father dead.

It surprised him that his father agreed to the younger brother's request, but he had to confess he was secretly glad to be rid of him. The family would no longer have to put up with the kid's disrespectful behavior, and as the only son left, he could finally have the full attention he deserved. Surely now his father would recognize the impeccable way he always did exactly what his father asked. As months turned into years, he increased his workload to make up for the heartbreak his brother had caused. Sadly, his father never seemed to shake the loss. His eyes never stopped wistfully gazing out the window to the road that led to their home.

Then one spring day, he heard his father yelp with an emotion he had never heard from him. In an unbridled childlike display of joy, he watched his father run wildly out the door, his arms flailing with delight. He couldn't help being slightly embarrassed as neighbors watched his father's exhibition and curiously peered down the road for what prompted it. When they recognized the figure on the road that his father was running toward, they shook their heads in disbelief. In an instant, the gossip mill had begun. He could not believe the horrific drama that was unfolding before his eyes.

To make matters worse, his father locked his brother in a full-court embrace and yelled out *in front of the neighborhood* that he did not even *need* to ask for forgiveness. The mangy rat was extolled rather than punished for squandering his father's inheritance and coming home broke. He couldn't look at either one of them as they made their way up the road, locked in a tearful embrace.

Had he done so, he would have seen that his brother's mud-covered face and tattered and stained clothes displayed his self-inflicted punishment. His brother had spent the last several months shoveling slop in a pigpen, miles away from the frivolous fun he had briefly enjoyed. But all he saw was the ostentatious display of unearned generosity. The unfairness of his father's actions incensed him, so he walked away to stew outside. He wanted no part of this joy, and he hoped his father would eventually come to his senses and give his brother the punishment he deserved.

Instead, his father killed the prized fatted calf and prepared a feast, and the injustice strangled him. *That was supposed to be mine*, he brooded to himself, and as people arrived to celebrate, he stayed in the distance outside. Watching them hug and toast and eat the prized beef, he was compulsively glued to the scene with longing. Uninvited tears began to gather in his eyes, so he jerked his face away and tried to distract himself with work.

He was startled when a hand grabbed his shoulder, and when he turned, a familiar bearded face was gazing at him. For a moment he softened, but when his dad began to implore him to join the party, he could not see past the injustice to hear his plea. "You are always with me, and everything I have is yours," his father cried out. "But we had to celebrate and be glad, because this brother of yours was dead and is alive again; he was lost...." His father's appeal continued, but he could no longer hear a sound. When his father said the word "celebrate," the words lost their volume and bumped up against a mountain of resentment deep inside his heart.

The word should have been "punish," not "celebrate," for what his brother had done in his lostness could never be returned. The way his dad washed over his brother's actions with undeserved grace seemed to discount the suffering they had endured because of him. But mostly, if he was honest, his dad's forgiveness undermined all that he had done and earned. In the silence he considered what it would mean to let go of his scale and move toward the relationships in front of him that were riddled with unfairness. The next step would be his—and he would have to climb over his need to get what he deserved to join in and bask in what was his.

The story of the prodigal son (Luke 15:11-32) is about the extravagance of grace, but when it is told from the perspective of the elder brother, it illustrates a core dilemma of what to do with imperfect relationships. Stepfamilies are full of them, and ultimately our choice is to embrace the family we have or to leave. Sometimes the bad seems to outweigh the good, and the temptation is great to remove ourselves.

Only you can determine if the bad is seasonal or destructive and what the course of action should be. Certainly, one option is to do as the elder brother did and remove ourselves—which brings an immediate relief to a situation or relationship that embitters us. But we need to look long and hard at what aspects of the situation are temporary, and what we'll lose if we don't stay.

Unfairness is a given in stepparenting; and I think the wedding vows of future stepfamilies should be altered to include it. Perhaps couples should consider responding to this phrase:

"For richer or for poorer, in sickness and in health, in unfairness and grace…Will you let go of what you deserve to be a part of the family you now join?"

Your answer to this question is similar to the choice that this older brother faces in the story. He has every right to remain outside, but he will be separated from his family—graceless and alone. Extending undeserved grace would be painful, but it would bring him the joy of connectedness and belonging. His brother might blow it again, he might see his dad taken advantage of many more times, and he might always have to do more than his share. He may feel the weight of holding too much in the family and have to learn to set his own boundaries. But he would experience the freedom of living without resentment, and he would no longer be serving with expectations of what he should get in return.

When we reduce our lives to fairness, we restrict ourselves from relationships that could bring us great joy if we could gather our Father's grace and use it as a blanket. That was the elder's son's opportunity, and the story leaves off with the father's offer to take his hand and accompany him inside. The story is unfinished on purpose and leaves us to determine what we will do in our battles of unfairness. Jesus originally told the story to woo people to consider the scandalous choice of trading legalism for grace. It's a painful trade if we, like the older brother, have lived "eye for an eye, and tooth for a tooth," holding fast to fairness. Only a recipient of undeserved grace understands what it means to extend it, so the father's imploring face is the offer in front of us all. My beloved professor says at the end of his book that if we choose to keep resentment alive, we are the ones who lose because it will continue to wound us. Conversely, when we forgive, we will not be doing it just for the person who hurt us; we will be doing it so we can be free.

Taking God's hand into our stepparenting, we are equipped with what we need to endure unfairness. His love is generous and abundant and there to cover us every time we run out. The older brother needs to go back over the words his father says and instead of focusing on the words about his brother, he needs to take in the words he says to him. If he does that, his story will end with "everything I have is yours" filling his heart and empowering his life.

Ours can too.

7

Finding Perspective

There are corners of our house that hold small collections of projects, pictures, and poems that I will never get rid of. They carry words and drawings from Jordan that give me oxygen for the days that are bereft. One of my favorites is a drawing he gave me in second grade that has never left its place on our refrigerator. It is a picture of a woman with a giant smile, a triangle nose, two cone feet, and outstretched arms. All these years later, that drawing still inspires me, especially when I'm in a rough moment in my stepparenting. That open-armed lady greets me when my face holds no smile, my stepson has an attitude, and I'm getting food out of the fridge with my hands clenched in a fist.

Another treasure I've kept is a card that came much later in my stepparenting. I keep it next to my computer—I am actually looking at it right now as I write. On the front of the card is a mama elephant with a baby owl curled in her trunk, and both of them are wearing glasses. The caption says, "Motherhood requires love, not DNA," and the only attribute Mama and her son share is what they are wearing on their eyes. Jordan signed the card "I'm so grateful to have you"—words I rarely hear from his mouth—so I've strategically placed this card where I can always see it. But this card also reminds me of my need to see beyond difficult moments, and the mama elephant's glasses are a symbol for my need.

My treasures from Jordan are scattered around our house to give me perspective during challenging seasons of stepparenting. If you have not kept any treasures from your stepchild, I recommend you start collecting or recording them regardless of how small or incidental they may be. To succeed in grace-filled stepparenting, we need to be able to shift our focus to something different from the circumstances in front of us. Even the smallest things can help us find the perspective we need when we want to give up.

Your perspective is foundational for your ability to stay the course in stepparenting. Perspective reminds us of the full story of our stepparenting journey rather than being stuck in what is happening now. As I write this chapter, my stepson and I have been trapped together for three months in the Coronavirus lockdown, and let's just say we are not in the most heartfelt juncture of our relationship. His driver's test was canceled, he is relegated to online school, and he's been sequestered with his parents when he should be in a season of enjoying more independence. As for me, lockdown with my seventeen-year-old stepson is not the most conducive environment for reflecting on the jewels of stepparenting. There have been moments when I lost it—and then came back to my computer to write advice I haven't been able to live. Suffice to say, grace is not just something we need for our stepchild—it's something we have to give ourselves because there are moments when we feel like failures. This chapter is written as much for me as it is for you—I need to remember that there is a bigger story happening than what I see in front of my eyes.

As stepparents, it's helpful to have a tool to find perspective in order to get a different view from the one we see. Like the glasses on the mama elephant, we need some lenses to get us through chapters of stepparenting that threaten to derail our course. Being able to pull back and look at our relationship with our stepchild from a broader perspective reminds us that we are in a chapter of a much bigger story. Discerning when to pull in and pay attention to something that might be happening now helps us not to miss gifts that can put wind in our sails. There are times when we need to look back and remember that what is currently going on with our stepchild could be affected by something that took place before us. And our greatest vision comes from being able to look up to God for what we need in painful seasons, knowing He'll give us the strength to fulfill our call.

The perspective you get from pulling back, pulling in, looking back, and looking up will strengthen you in your stepparenting by revealing your trajectory from a different angle. These views are represented by four lenses I introduced in a book called *When Changing Nothing Changes Everything*, and they can help you find perspective during bleak stepparenting seasons. In this chapter, I will show you some ways to access and use these lenses by sharing stories of how I've used them in my stepparenting. These lenses can give you the vision to see past the hopelessness of certain seasons and empower you with enough strength to stay your course.

WHAT TO SEE THROUGH

A young stepfather had just begun his life with his new bride, and he was looking for ways to bond with his new stepdaughter. Even though she was just a toddler, he had read enough to know she needed to go at her own pace to welcome him into her heart. He wanted to let her lead as much as possible in building the intimacy of their relationship. So when he saw her toddling toward him with a small tray and clear intentions, he grabbed the remote and turned off the TV so he would be entirely hers.

"Time for tea," she announced, and he knew this was his moment. She put the tray down on the coffee table and held out a mini cup filled with water, and the two of them ate pretend cookies while they sipped.

When they finished, she slid off the couch and carried the tray down the hall toward her bedroom. He was filled with what the moment meant for his heart.

Then it suddenly dawned on him. *Where would a toddler get water to fill a cup for tea?* When he followed her down the hall and inquired, she took his hand and walked toward the toilet. A slight wave of nausea interrupted his delight.

As stepparents, we may have to look past (or swallow) a little toilet water in order to see the big picture in our relationship with our stepchild. Our perspective not only determines where we focus but also guides our responses to our stepchildren because of how we interpret what we see. If the young stepfather focused on the fact that he just imbibed some toilet water, he might have reprimanded his stepdaughter rather than appreciate her overture toward him. He would have missed what was happening in their relationship because he was fixated on the water in his tea. A negative response would be unlikely in this situation because of the age of the little girl, but it can easily happen in less adorable situations. We miss what is actually happening in our relationship with our stepchild when we allow the wrong details to shape what we see.

Jesus speaks about the importance of perspective in Matthew 6:22 when he says, "The eye is the lamp of the body. If your eyes are healthy, your whole body will be full of light." He says these words in the context of temptation, but He makes the point that where you focus your eyes will influence what happens next. He advises that turning your eyes a different direction (or in His very dramatic words, removing them) can stop you from being led into temptation. Conversely, the more you focus on what is tempting you, the more likely you are to fall.

This truth can be applied in many situations with your stepchildren (except the part about removing your eyes). Being able to shift your focus tempers your response, and the way you respond *can* make a difference in how your story unfolds. In my survey, stepparents said responding to their stepchildren with unconditional love during extremely tough times made a difference, though they didn't always immediately see it. You and your stepchild are writing a long story, and your actions and responses in difficult seasons will shape how that story unfolds.

You can see through your present circumstances to the big picture with what I call the "big-view lens." You access this perspective by imagining yourself looking through a microscope at your stepchild and then pulling away. You are suddenly reminded that you are looking at a miniscule particle of an evolving story. Seeing the big picture of your stepparenting can guide your response to something that is happening in front of you right now. It helps you discern what you may need to overlook.

When I was first bonding with Jordan, I noticed that occasionally he would distance himself from me. Other times he would draw me near. Instead of taking it personally and reacting when I felt rejected, I saw it as part of the process of him accepting another mother into his life. The big view of Jordan's grief, separation, and bonding helped me not to look at any single situation as the full story. I learned to savor moments when he held me close and keep those moments in my heart, while I allowed him space when he was distant. I needed to give him time to acclimate and heal.

The big view also helps you see how your actions right now contribute to the bigger story. Your response of grace toward your stepchild might feel small right now, but it could be the beginning of something much bigger down the road. Remembering my own young stepmom's restraint during those dinner-table conversations when we left her out, I realize now the power of her graciousness. At the time I barely noticed it, but I've gained a fuller perspective of her sacrifice as years have gone by. This has been a clear illustration to me that part of being a stepparent is trusting that my unappreciated actions and responses will someday be noticed. Even if Jordan doesn't remember a specific event or circumstance, he will one day view the way I responded to him throughout our relationship through adult eyes.

In this chapter of my stepparenting—Jordan's teenage years and writing this book—I find I continually need to pull back and look at the bigger story. The big-view lens allows me to see Jordan's current behavior as part of an evolving story rather than the way our relationship will always be. During these COVID months I have taken many walks—much-needed moments away from our house—so I will hold my tongue. Other times I haven't had as much self-control, and I've blurted out things (and heard back things from Jordan) that drive me to look at my collection of treasures to survive. My voice is often dim (and unwanted) in his current state of maturity. But this is an opportunity for me to understand what many stepparents feel for much longer periods of time. It's also a chance for me to see if the tools I am writing about in this chapter actually work.

However, even in this challenging season, there have been a few moments I've savored; and I've learned to raise the volume of those moments to keep them locked in my memory. It takes a trained ear and eye to know when to stop and do that, and you may have to set the bar low to grab them when they come. It may mean merely acknowledging when a negative behavior doesn't happen. Or perhaps when you asked your stepchild to do something, his response was slightly better than before. This ability to notice something happening in the present is the lens that allows us to pull in, and that is the one we turn to next.

WHEN TO PULL IN

In my current season with Jordan of grunts and rolled eyes, I was surprised by a short text that held a treasure for me to savor. Jordan asked me for the name of the publisher of one of my books. When I asked him why he needed it, he said he quoted me in one of his papers. Just to give you some context, a few hours earlier we had a much less amiable text exchange because he had spent multiple hours playing video games instead of studying for finals. I couldn't resist giving him my two cents, so our communication went something like this:

ME: "I'm praying you will make better choices than playing video games and fight for yourself in your studies."

JORDAN: "And I'm praying you'll not always be pressuring me to do stuff. Thanks."

That gives you a sense of the climate, so when I got that text from him asking for my publisher, it was a surprising stream in a desert. Instead of brushing past it, I savored it and let it color every disdainful tone of voice, helping me keep my eyes on the prize ahead. With all the snippiness between us during this season, this short overture helped me know I haven't lost my ground with him. It gave me wind in my sails to hold on through this time and know that we *will* pass through it. Our relationship will one day be different from what it is right now.

I share this scene to give you an idea of when to pull in—to see something that is happening in the present—and let it feed you. Most of the time as stepparents we need to keep our eye on the big picture, rather than an individual moment, to help us survive. However, part of surviving the stepparent journey is discerning when to pull in and put an exclamation point on something small that might be happening. Recording those moments or displaying reminders of them around your house can help you see the good during a season with your step-child that feels bleak.

Pulling in your focus in stepparenting is a little like reading a book and coming to a sentence that you underline or highlight. The rest of the page around that sentence is part of the story, but the part you see when you look back at the page is the sentence you made stand out. Our choices about where to focus can alter our stepparenting story. And the places we choose to focus have a direct bearing on what we do next.

When I got that edgy text from Jordan about his prayer that I would leave him alone, you can imagine I considered many responses to his attitude. Instead I put on my tennis shoes and texted back: "Your prayers were answered because I'm leaving for a walk." Sometimes the best way to survive a bad moment is to leave it. Take some time for yourself and remember your trajectory in your stepparenting. Don't let the bad moment shape your response to your stepchild, because you might regret it when something different and wonderful happens next.

When Jordan texted me hours later for the publisher of my book, I realized how quickly things can change in your stepparenting relationship. I knew not to overreact with joy (which would disgust him), but like Mary in Luke 2:19, I treasured his words and pondered them in my heart. It wasn't a huge deal, but I made it one because I feed off those moments in this current season. Taking note of the little things your stepchild says or does—even if they only indicate a miniscule relational advancement—can feed your soul in seasons like that too.

These first two lenses help you overlook some things and savor others. When you can discern when to pull out and when to pull in, you can focus on what is most important. Your response won't be dictated by every up and down circumstance. However, you need a third lens when things are happening that elude your understanding. When your stepchild is responding in a way that has nothing to do with what is going on in your present circumstances, something from your stepchild's past may be causing his present behavior. In times like this, the rearview lens helps you get the clarity you need.

ACCESSING YOUR STEPCHILD'S BACKSTORY

Remember the story I told you about Jordan's dog Kaya in chapter 2? If you don't, I caught you skimming, and now you'll have to look back to that chapter if you want to know what the story is. Looking back might actually be an appropriate exercise because that is exactly what this lens of stepparenting requires. The kind of looking back you need is knowing some of your stepchild's backstory, and what he or she went through before you arrived. When Jordan cried for Kaya after we married, Jere and I saw that his tears seemed to indicate something more was happening. We knew that his tears for the dog were because of sadness he felt because his family was no longer together. Knowing the story of the family dog helped us understand his grief.

This fuller story is something you should know when coming into a relationship with your stepchild. Otherwise, if you don't know what has transpired before you, you will be tempted to take every situation at face value and not have grace or understanding for what they say or do. Knowing your stepchild's backstory will give you insights into their behavior that might puzzle, anger, or hurt you.

Your stepchildren grieve the way their family has been restructured and all the ways that has complicated their lives. If there is any separation or loss with a biological parent, your stepchild might deal with abandonment issues that you have to absorb even though they have nothing to do with you. If your stepchild was formerly an oldest or youngest child and now has a different birth order in your stepfamily, they may spill out anger or confusion in their behavior. These are some of the issues that can surface in your stepparenting, and without accessing some rearview wisdom, these things cause unnecessary resentment or anger that can create a rift.

Author Wednesday Martin shares how her relationship with her stepdaughters was affected by dynamics they brought into the family from what happened before her. Her backstory helped her understand her own resentment (see chapter 3), but knowing her stepdaughters' backstory helped her understand some other dynamics taking place. Because her husband was single for a few years after his divorce, his daughters had grown accustomed to his full attention. That contributed to their reluctance to share him and accept her into the mix. Knowing more about the story she entered, she didn't take their behavior toward her quite as personally. She was also able to take the steps needed to protect her heart. After she tried to make a special meal for her stepdaughters and they complained about it not being quite right, she made the decision to let her husband cook for them to avoid unnecessary resentment.[1] Eventually, as her relationship with them grew more solid and they could talk through their feelings, having a fuller perspective helped her find ways to cope. Ms. Martin's stepdaughters eventually realized why they behaved the way they did, which is something many stepchildren (including me) experience through maturity. But the rear view helps you cope with dynamics you are currently experiencing in your stepparenting, knowing some things will become clear when your stepchild is able to see things from a new light.

The rear view of your stepchild's behavior can be informed by your spouse, so it's important to ask questions about your child's past when you begin stepparenting. Because your spouse has been with your child longer, he or she will have information about your child's story that you don't have. Remember that your spouse may have not done much thinking about your child's experience or dynamics from the past that could be related to the current behavior you are experiencing. You may be journeying together into that discovery, and your questions could unlock helpful insights for you both.

When Jordan first started crying for Kaya, Jere didn't understand why he was crying, but as we talked, we both came to a deeper understanding. We knew Jordan's mother's move to Australia would also eventually have an impact on him, and this prepared us for what he has experienced as a teenager in trying to understand the sadness in his heart. All these things come to you on a plate that you never knew you were getting when you say "I do" as a brand-new spouse and stepparent. Having the rear view helps you see the "why" of so much that happens in your child's behavior as you make your way through your stepparenting and try to map the best course.

As you log more years being a parent, the rear view eventually grows to include the part you play in your child's story. The story you entered was formed before you arrived, but now you are helping shape that story because of your presence in your stepchild's life. It may take time, understanding, and patience to wade through some of the difficulty you inherited. But one day your stepchildren's lives will include the chapters you lived with them, and who they ultimately become will partly be because of you. That is the perfect lead-in to the last lens to help you stay your course.

ABSORBING THE BAD FOR THE GOOD

The last lens that can help you in your stepparenting is the ability to look up to God for the perspective you need to do what is in front of you. Years ago, I read a story called "Ragman" that beautifully illustrates the strength God gives us in the power we get through Jesus's life. Ragman is an allegory about Jesus that affected me in a way I've never forgotten. And rereading it as a stepparent, I am aware of a new way of understanding this story for the mission and purpose of our role. As we consider this last lens of perspective in stepparenting, I believe an excerpt of this story is the best way to illustrate the God's-eye view of our call.

"New rags for old!" the Ragman cries out at the beginning of the story.

"I take your tired rags," he says, and you are pulled into the story as the narrator begins to follow him down the road. Here is what ensues after the narrator follows the Ragman's curious cries:

> I followed him. My curiosity drove me. And I wasn't disappointed.
>
> Soon the Ragman saw a woman sitting on her back porch. She was sobbing into a handkerchief, sighing, and shedding a thousand tears. Her knees and elbows made a sad X. Her shoulders shook. Her heart was breaking.
>
> The Ragman stopped his cart. Quietly, he walked to the woman, stepping round tin cans, dead toys, and Pampers.
>
> "Give me your rag," he said so gently, "and I'll give you another."
>
> He slipped the handkerchief from her eyes. She looked up, and he laid across her palm a linen cloth so clean and new that it shined. She blinked from the gift to the giver.

> Then, as he began to pull his cart again, the Ragman did a strange thing: he put her stained handkerchief to his own face; and then he began to weep, to sob as grievously as she had done, his shoulders shaking. Yet she was left without a tear.

The story continues as the Ragman encounters other people. But it's his encounter with a child that pierced my stepparent heart. Perhaps it will pierce yours too.

> In a little while, when the sky showed grey behind the rooftops and I could see the shredded curtains hanging out black windows, the Ragman came upon a girl whose head was wrapped in a bandage, whose eyes were empty. Blood soaked her bandage. A single line of blood ran down her cheek.
>
> Now the tall Ragman looked upon this child with pity, and he drew a lovely yellow bonnet from his cart.
>
> "Give me your rag," he said, tracing his own line on her cheek, "and I'll give you mine."
>
> The child could only gaze at him while he loosened the bandage, removed it, and tied it to his own head. The bonnet he set on hers. And I gasped at what I saw: for with the bandage went the wound! Against his brow it ran a darker, more substantial blood—his own!
>
> "Rags! Rags! I take old rags!" cried the sobbing, bleeding, strong, intelligent Ragman.
>
> The sun hurt both the sky, now, and my eyes.[2]

The story of the Ragman continues on after this excerpt, and the narrator follows him as he takes the rags of a jobless man as well as an alcoholic. As he exchanges rags with the people in his path, he continues to take on their painful circumstances and bear them so they can be healed. It is an allegory of what Jesus does for us and the power we have through His life to do the same for others. In stepparenting, we are given that opportunity as we absorb our child's sorrows.

I stopped the story when the Ragman confronts the bleeding child, as I feel it speaks powerfully to the role we play as stepparents. Our children aren't bleeding physically, but they carry brokenness inwardly, and we can be a part of their healing by absorbing their grief. Their bloody rag may come out in anger or in resentment or in treating you in a way you don't deserve, but when you stand in the gap, you secure your place as a parent who is called to them. The Ragman can hold the rags you can't handle, and His strength allows you to participate in your stepchild's healing and make a difference in their adult life.

This is the higher view. It represents the view of God we have as Christ-followers—that our stepparenting is a call that God has given us. When we stand in the gap for our stepchildren, we absorb things that are unfair and difficult, and we contribute better things to their lives. We may never get the appreciation or acknowledgement we deserve, but we can participate in the "unfair love" God has given us. And our ability to look up and get the strength we need during overwhelming seasons is what helps us see our calling through.

A FINAL WORD ON PERSPECTIVE

"Now we see in a mirror, dimly," Paul writes in 1 Corinthians 13:12 (NRSV), "but then we will see face to face." He goes on to say, "Now I know only in part; then I will know fully," which indicates that our vision is partially impaired. We can't see all that is actually happening around us, so we need to find perspective to persevere while we live out our calling. We may not ever see the power of all our actions, but Paul indicates that a day will come when we will see more of what is happening now. It may take months, years, or a lifetime to see the result of our sacrifices. But God keeps these things in His treasure box, and this passage indicates that everything we've been and are is fully known.

Sometimes we have to see through what is immediately before us and to know that our actions and responses are part of a bigger story. As we persist in being patient, kind, humble, and forgiving, something is happening in our stepchildren that we can't always see with the limited view before our eyes. Having some inward lenses that we can "put on" gives us a new focus when we are trying to make it through a difficult chapter. And one day, 1 Corinthians 13 says, we will see clearly what we now only see in part.

The mama elephant and baby owl on my Mother's Day card have become my symbols of a stepchild and stepparent seeing the gift they have in each other. Their glasses speak to me of how they are able to see the unique place they hold in each other's lives. Until a stepparent and stepchild see all that happens in their story, they won't fully understand the value of their relationship. Until then, the card reminds me to wear the lenses I need for every moment I have parenting Jordan, because those moments shape my call.

8

Advice from the Trenches

In the past seven chapters, you've read many of the things I've learned about stepparenting. In this chapter I thought it would be beneficial to share some wise words from other stepparent voices. Because my story is only one story of stepparenting, I wanted to include other voices about how they navigated their stepparenting journey. In my survey, I asked them to share one piece of advice they would give to other stepparents. Their advice was so good, I decided to give them a chapter of their own. So get out your highlighter—this chapter will be the one you'll return to for quick help in your stepparenting. Here are fifteen tips from the 125 stepparents I surveyed to help you navigate stepparenting life:

You can never really blend two families. You are creating a new, different family together.

When you become a stepparent, you quickly discover that the term "blended family" is a bit of a misnomer. You are not blending two families—you are creating a new family. It includes a bridge to your child's other family that allows your child to comfortably travel back and forth. If both you and your spouse come into your marriage with children, your family will need two bridges, and you will also have changing sibling dynamics to navigate. These changes need to be piloted without expectation of what your relationships *should* look like, because they will take on a unique life of their own. Everyone needs to feel they have a part in creating your family, not being forced into a family picture you and your spouse may have or a closeness they are not ready for. Ron Deal's analogy that a stepfamily is cooked in a Crock-Pot and that no two dishes (or families) are exactly the same reminds us of the patience and endurance it takes to build a new home.

The most important thing is for you and your spouse to be a team.

Because I devoted much of chapter 2 to this, I won't say much more, but I am including it because of how important this is in stepparenting. Your spouse is *the* major player in your stepparenting success, and he or she will largely determine your long-term place in your stepchild's life. My husband was a stepparent in his previous marriage, and because his ex-wife positioned him as co-parent, his place in his stepchildren's hearts was secure even after their marriage ended. Jere still has a close relationship with them, and they still think of him as their father even though both of them are now adults. When you marry a parent, the partnership you establish in parenting your kids helps you navigate your relationship with them. Because your spouse has the more permanent biological bond, his or her support in your parenting will determine the role you will have in your stepchild's life. The relationship my husband built with his stepchildren grew even to include me after I came into his life.

What you say and do now will pay dividends down the road.

One way to think about approaching your stepparenting is that you are making deposits into your "parenting bank account" during your first few years as a stepparent. You may not feel like much is progressing in your relationship, but you are slowly growing relational capital with your child. They will remember the things you say and do even when they seem to go unnoticed, and your words and actions may grow to be really important in your child's development. However, you may need to bear through times when you don't get the acknowledgment or response you deserve, knowing you will reap the benefits of your actions further down the road. The reward will come from seeing how your deposits help shape your stepchild's health and growth.

The other side of this advice is what you *don't* do or say—particularly about your stepchild's other parent or family—will also pay dividends. The discipline you have in withholding negative feelings or responses in front of your stepchildren will create the most peaceful environment for them to find their own way. When your stepchildren become adults, they will have a much fuller perspective on all the dynamics of their parents and family. Until then, you may have to stay silent, so they can come into their own understanding as they grow. Putting your stepchild in the middle of a conflict between parents makes an already stressful situation even worse, so sacrificing your need to vent may be your most courageous and important act as a stepparent. Otherwise your child will be forced to defend and protect what they may one day see differently for themselves.

Keep your expectations low (or better yet, don't have any at all!), but keep your hopes high.

I love this advice because it reveals the challenge that stepparenting is but leaves room for what God can do with it. It also sets expectations apart from hope, which offers a helpful distinction for what to let go of and what to hold. Expectations can be deadly because your stepfamily will almost certainly *not* evolve the way you picture it. Whether it is in the length of time things take, or the amount of challenges you face, there will be bumps in the road that will interrupt your vision of how things should unfold. The best picture to have of the way your stepfamily will evolve is an empty frame waiting to be filled.

Holding hope, however, is an entirely different thing than having expectations. Expectations are specific things you want to happen; hope is a promise that good things *will* happen even though you don't know what those things are. God gives us hope as we observe what He is doing, trusting that He sees more than we do and has bigger plans than we can imagine. God is at work in every life in your stepfamily, so each person is experiencing their own unique journey, and that will influence the way things evolve. Things always take more time than we think, and this is especially true in the dynamics of stepfamilies. Your relationships will grow and change in ways you might not be able to imagine right now. Never let go of your hope—it is what keeps you knowing that with time and love, good things will eventually happen. It also gives you the vision and strength to watch and wait for what those things are.

Remember that children are not responsible for adult issues.

This advice should be underlined as your filter every time you are tempted to bring your frustrations with your child's other family into your stepparenting. Simply said, anything negative that you experience with your stepchild's other parents should not be carried into your interactions with your child. You may think this advice sounds easy, but many parents fall into this temptation when it comes to shared parenting. The child can easily be placed in the middle and have to absorb feelings or actions between parents that they should not have to broker, absorb, or defend. If you have a tough co-parenting situation, it may be difficult not to carry resentment over to your children from issues you have with the bio parent. If this is the case, find a friend or a counselor outside the home to sort your feelings out so you can approach your parenting with a clean slate.

Your child may also have mannerisms or personality traits that are similar to a parent you have problems with, and this can cause you to inadvertently transfer feelings about them onto your stepchild. Consciously separating what belongs (or doesn't belong) to your stepchildren will help you parent more clearly and maturely, and not say or do things you might later regret. Remember that once something is said out loud, it can never be unsaid, so you will never regret choosing your words carefully. Restraint is one of your best allies in stepparenting, and you can rest assured that whatever is happening right now will be seen from a much fuller perspective when your child grows up.

Hang in there—even biological parents sometimes think their children don't like them.

Right after I wrote these words, I received a text from my teenage stepson that implied I was an idiot. Of course, he didn't use the word "idiot," but you could hear it in his tone when he explained why my text was unnecessary because he already knew everything I wrote. As a stepparent, it's good to remember that some of your challenges with your stepkids are universal parenting issues. When kids are in their teenage years, anyone who is parenting them (biological or not) is going to get their fill of "I knows," accompanied by disdainful looks and rolled eyes. Rather than seeing their behavior as rejection, look at it from the angle that they are familiar enough with you to treat you the same way they would treat a biological parent.

Teenagers are moving toward independence, and if you are the one parenting them, you will find yourself in the eye of the "I don't need you because I know everything" storm. The tone of Jordan's text was painfully similar to a tone I used regularly to my parents when I was a teenager. I still can hear the phrase "Your attitude, young lady..." because it was repeated to me more times than I can count. Part of all teenagers' rite of passage is to irritate their parents so much that the parents aren't too sad when they send them off to college. If you have a role in parenting during this time, you will have to absorb some kind of attitude as part of their growth. Because of my years in youth ministry,

Jordan's text made me laugh and recognize this was part of being a parent of a teenager. I could even see good in it (but don't tell him) because it revealed that he felt familiar enough with me to treat me as a true mom in his life. You can see it this way too.

Be yourself.

These two words seem so simple, yet when it comes to stepparenting, they are surprisingly difficult to live out. The pressure to be liked can cause you to be who your stepchild might want you to be instead of who you are. At the beginning of the book, I said that stepparenting is like standing on the edge of a pool filled with people and deciding how you will enter. Not only do you have to choose how far you'll dive in, but you have the additional pressure of winning over the child who is the focus of everyone there.

With the weight you feel to be liked, you may be tempted to be someone different from who you are in order to gain your stepchild's favor. To embrace the call of stepparenting is to trust that *you* are the one called to your stepchild's life. *Who you are* is the person God will use in your stepfamily. Your particular strengths and personality traits will provide unique guidance and encouragement in your stepchild's life.

This truth has played out with Jordan and me through our strong wills (which we both have) as well as our similar emotional makeup. Jordan and I are both fours on the Enneagram, so we share a capacity to feel a range of emotions and moods that can either overwhelm us or lead to creative success. Because of this common temperament, I relate in a unique way to some of what he goes through, and I can see God's design in bringing us together. Though we don't share the same biology, God has used our similar emotional makeup as a bridge for me to understand Jordan, and we can learn from each other in a way that enriches both our lives.

The bottom line is, don't try to be someone else to win over your stepchildren, because there is something you alone have to give them.

You are the one God brought to love and care for your stepchild, and He has a plan to use you in ways that will continue to unfold.

Take life one day at a time.

As I've said in previous chapters, this is not the way I naturally live, but I believe it's the life God wants for us (see Matthew 6:34). The phrase "one day at a time" says in a nutshell the biggest lesson God has used stepparenting to teach me. I've been stretched to become flexible and have learned (sometimes kicking and screaming) to accept circumstances constantly changing. It's not that you can't make any plans as a stepparent; you just have to hold them loosely and put them beneath the well-being of your child. Your relationship with your stepchild may cost you convenience, but your sacrifices will bring you and your stepchild closer. What you achieve relationally by accommodating the plan given to you is often better than what you get when you hold stubbornly to the plan you make.

This advice to take life one day at a time is not just for schedules—it's also the way to approach your relationships with your stepchildren. You may go through one or two (or ten) rough seasons, but don't let those seasons define your stepparenting course. Things will continue to evolve, and it may it take many months and years for change to happen. The rough spots you are going through now are part of how a trusting relationship is formed. Live the circumstances in front of you today the best that you can, knowing that your commitment and consistency could bring a shift tomorrow. Taking life one day at a time leaves room for what God will do, and the way things look right now could be very different from how things end up.

"One day at a time" is not only the mantra of stepparents and recovery groups, it is a theme Jesus emphasizes to His followers in Matthew 6. He says in His Sermon on the Mount that life is meant to be lived in the present, because when we live in the future, we are often plagued with worry and fear. Perhaps that is why God refers to Himself as "I am" in Exodus 3:14, when He is assuring Moses of His presence with him in the future. God dwells with us moment by moment, and when we try to imagine what's to come, we project ourselves to a place He hasn't brought us to yet. God is doing things right now in you and your stepchild that He doesn't want you to miss.

Be forgiving. Stepkids say hurtful things they don't really mean.

One thing you will want to put away for good in your stepparenting is your mental tape recorder. You will experience scenes and conversations that will be best for you to forget for the health and progression of your stepfamily relationships. You may want to go back to chapter 6 and read more detailed words about the power of grace and forgiveness in stepparenting as you take in this advice. Some things are meant to be forgotten, and that leaves room for the words and conversations that are meant to never leave your heart. Choosing what to remember and what to forget is the way to stepparent with grace.

Another important insight to remember is that the hurtful things your stepkids say to you, particularly at the beginning of your relationship, will likely have nothing to do with you. They are often due to the pain of their family's dissolution and their parents' failed marriage. Depending on their age and the circumstances of your stepfamily, you may have to weather some verbal storms. You and your spouse may need to set boundaries for your stepchild's behavior, but knowing there is more underneath their actions gives you a margin of grace for how to respond. It also protects your heart for your future with your stepchild because you know the hurtful things they do or say have more to do with their situation than what they feel about you. Separating yourself from what gets projected onto you will require discernment, tenacity, and strength. You will probably face those things better if you are intentional about getting support.

The more you let go of the bad, the more attention you will be able to give to the good progress that might be happening. Conversely, when you hold on to the bad, you are less likely to see the good, and that may hinder your relationship. Your expectations for your relationship with your stepchildren can become self-fulfilling prophecies—negatively because of the tension you hold on to, or positively because of the grace you extend to them. As a stepparent, you have more power than you know to shape the way your relationship with your stepchild unfolds.

Discerning when you need to press "erase" is a skill every stepparent needs—and some need to do it more frequently than others. If you are one of them, mark this piece of advice and reread it as often as you need to not let hurtful things steer your love.

Marriages influence adult stepchildren too.

You may think once children leave the nest, parents are free to do whatever they want in their relationships. I can tell you from personal experience that second marriages do have an impact on adult children. If you come into a marriage where your spouse has grown children, it's important to consider their feelings and expectations about their parent marrying you. Loving your spouse includes committing to your spouse's family, and just because their children aren't under your roof doesn't mean they are not part of your life. The decisions you make about where to live, spend holidays, or vacation should include (at least in part) a consideration of your adult stepchildren and their families. Otherwise you and your spouse will be neglecting the relationships that could be increasingly meaningful and important as you age.

Stepparents of adult children have more power over the kind of relationship their spouse has with his or her children. Because visits are chosen rather than required, you can work to support your spouse in those relationships or allow those relationships to grow distant or detached. Your spouse probably has more loyalty to you than to his or her adult children because there is less regular interaction with them. You are more a part of your spouse's day-to-day life than they are, so the relationships you build together with others will grow to define your life. When you make an effort to build strong relationships with your spouse's adult children, you enrich your marriage and future by investing in your spouse's family life.

On a positive note, it is often easier for stepparents to be grafted into grandparent status because most children don't care (or even know) if a grandparent is related to them biologically. Grandparents win simply by being present in their grandchildren's lives. The time and care you invest in your spouse's children and grandchildren will carve a loving place for you in your stepfamily. And the more people you can find room to love, the bigger your family becomes.

Love unconditionally regardless of whether the child wants you to. They will notice.

These words are so important, I am going to ask you to stop right now and reread them. I feel like Moses in Deuteronomy 11:18—these are words you want to tie as symbols on your hands and bind to your foreheads because they are so important in your stepparenting life. Your unconditional love is the one thing in your arsenal that you have complete control of in your stepfamily. Many circumstances of your stepparenting are not in your control, but this is the one thing no one else can control that you have the power to give. It is the most powerful force you have to make a lasting impact in your stepchild. When you are the target of someone's unconditional love, it has a way of wrapping around your heart and can redirect your life.

Children of divorced parents carry that brokenness deep in their hearts because the relationship that formed them is no longer a firm foundation. That relationship has been blown apart by a decision they didn't make, and they are left to pay the cost. Even when loving and supportive relationships have been brought to them through their parent's remarriage, it is natural for them to be angry, suspicious, or defended. These feelings have nothing to do with you, but they can influence your stepparenting life. Your ability to love in the face of rejection will not only be an example to them but could also be your greatest contribution to their healing and growth.

Extending this love requires some discernment, as it is given in different forms depending on how close you are in your relationship. Communicating it quietly through your actions can be more effective than proclaiming it enthusiastically during certain times. The most important thing to remember is that your consistency gives unconditional love its force. Ask God for the grace to keep on loving your stepchild even if that love appears to go unnoticed. Perhaps the reason you are there is so God can use your love to powerfully alter the future of a human life.

This is a marathon, not a sprint.

I deeply regret that I never had the experience of running a marathon. I jogged for twenty-five years, but because I did it for exercise, I never pushed myself to do a race. However, one time I did run eleven miles, and it gave me a peek into what it takes to go the distance. You have to settle into a long-term mentality and find a rhythm in order to finish at a steady pace. You also have to prepare to "hit the wall"—something runners dread that happens when you reach your limit. It is described as a similar feeling to running headlong into a pile of bricks—your legs feel like concrete posts, and your mind starts to question whether there is a finish line at all.

That is actually a pretty good description of what stepparenting can feel like. There are times when you are so beaten down, you feel like you've hit the wall and just want to quit. However, exercise physiologist Dr. Tim Noakes says you can overcome hitting the wall if you have tools for perseverance. He says that even when a voice whispers in your ear that you've given all you've got to give, in reality, it is possible to dig deeper and give more.[1]

Noakes gives three tips for what to do when you hit the wall in running that I believe apply to stepparenting:

Find a way to distract yourself. Distractions help runners focus on something not associated with the race. For stepparents, that can translate to getting away with a friend or a spouse and doing something apart from your parenting. Have moments when you separate yourself from your role and nurture the other parts of who you are.

Believe you can overcome your hurdle. Runners can do this through visualization, self talk, or faith. For stepparents, remembering that God has called you to the task of parenting this child helps you know that He will give you what it takes to see it through.

Have a running partner who can accompany you to the end. You need someone alongside you who can push you past the wall in your stepparenting relationships. This can be your support group, a friend, or your spouse. Letting someone else know when you feel you can't go on allows them to come alongside you and give you the encouragement you need to keep going to the end.

Your role as stepparent will last a lifetime, so you need to approach your stepparenting as a marathon. Though the active parenting years are undoubtedly the most consuming, your relationship with your stepchild will continue in some form for the rest of your life. Pace yourself with the hope and faith that even in the last mile, things can happen that make the whole race worth it. And just like runners who start out in the middle of the pack but come on strong at the finish, you may experience delightful surprises all the way to the end.

This is not a competition with the biological mom or dad.

One of the biggest challenges for any parent is learning how to share your children. Whether you are a biological parent, adoptive parent, or stepparent, you will feel this challenge at various stages of your child's life. In stepfamilies, you learn up front what all parents experience when their child grows up and leaves them. The more you can share your children with others who love them, the more space their love for you has to grow.

I sometimes hear from stepparents, "The biological mom isn't really a mom at all," or "The biological dad is not really present." Even if that is true in your situation, you still need to honor the biological parent's place in your child's life. Regardless of the way they parent, they are a huge part of your stepchild's heart and life. Even if they are deceased, their presence will continue to be missed as your child grows and develops. If your child feels forced to choose between you and the biological parent, it can create stress in their life that you have the power to resolve. Supporting your stepchildren by securing a biological parent's place only increases your closeness. There is room in a child's heart for any adult who offers love and support, and stepping in without competition is the best way to win their love and live your call.

Join a support group—or start one.

Through my survey, I have become aware of many stepparenting support groups, and it was clear these groups were not just helpful but lifesaving. Having someone to talk to who is going through the same challenges provides you with help and encouragement when you feel like you want to quit. Support groups have been successful for getting people through addiction, helping people hang on to their faith, and providing opportunities to help other people, which mysteriously brings you healing. Many passages of Scripture affirm that community is essential to our health and faith and that we are meant to face our challenges with others, not alone (see Romans 12:15, 1 Corinthians 12, and Galatians 6:2, for example). Having other stepparents in your life who know what you are going through can bring health and perspective to your particular journey. God has given us the gift of each other, and He declared from the beginning that it is not good for any of us to be on our own (Genesis 2:18).

Get counseling when you need it.

Maybe it's because my mother was a therapist, but I've always been an advocate for counseling. Some see it as a sign of weakness, but I think most people now agree it is actually a sign of great strength. Getting some deeper help will not only help you get through a specific problem but also help you see what is behind that problem that you may be able to do differently. Chapter 5 talks about the inside job of stepparenting, and this advice to get counseling when needed fits with much of what that chapter conveys. Whether you decide to get counseling individually or as a couple, any professional help you receive will only make you a better stepparent. The insights that come from counseling can provide tools and knowledge that bolster your stepparenting because of how they work to change you.

Don't give up.

I planned to quote Winston Churchill's three-word speech "Never give up" for the perfect end of this chapter. However, a quick online search revealed that this is an edited version of the speech he actually gave. What Churchill *did* say still provides great encouragement for us to grab ahold of in our stepparenting. So with the words that Churchill spoke at Harrow School in 1941, I give you this chapter's final stepparenting charge:

> Never give in, never give in, never, never, never, never—in nothing great or small, large or petty—never give in except to convictions of honor and good sense. Never yield to force; never yield to the apparently overwhelming might of the enemy. We stood all alone a year ago, and to many countries it seemed that our account was closed, we were finished…
>
> But instead our country stood in the gap. There was no flinching and no thought of giving in; and by what seemed almost a miracle to those outside these Islands, though we ourselves never doubted it, we now find ourselves in a position where I can say that we can be sure that we have only to persevere to conquer.[2]

Churchill's actual speech is even better than the three-word one I heard about; it describes in needed detail what it takes to persevere when all appears to be lost. There will be times in your stepparenting where you will feel a stake in what Great Britain went through in the battle of World War II—when it appeared their nation would be overpowered and crushed. The next chapter shows what happens when you hold on through the obstacles. By doing so, you will witness what God can do.

9

Stories of Hope

I believe the greatest encouragement stepparents can receive is a real-life story that breathes hope into their journey. In this chapter I have included five of them, and each story reveals a different angle of what God can do with the broken chapters of our lives. The first story is of a single man who became a stepfather to four girls—with six generations of only males in his family history. The second is about a woman who married a young widower after he was left with two children when cancer abruptly took his first wife. You'll be introduced to a couple who became friends after their spouses had an affair—and now are celebrating twenty years of marriage. A woman who never dreamed her husband would leave her was scooped up in her brokenness by God's redemption when a new man prayed her into his life. And finally, you'll meet a couple who are still in the middle of their story and see how they have found a way to hold on to hope.

These are brave and redemptive stories, and I felt honored to hear them. I am also grateful to have their permission to share them with you. These stepparents made the courageous decision to let their stories be included because they wanted to pour their encouragement to persevere into your souls. Perhaps one of them will speak especially to you.

EARL

When Earl started dating a woman with four daughters, three of the girls welcomed him into the family. The oldest daughter went to live with her father, and because the separation was still fresh, she and Earl didn't have a chance to form more than an acquaintance after she left. The three younger daughters, however, made Earl their "human tree," regularly jumping into his arms when he arrived for visits and becoming instantly devoted to him. Earl realized the biological dad had left holes in all four girls' hearts, and because he knew he would never be able to fill those holes completely, his journey continues to bring him joy and heartache at every stage of his stepfather life.

Earl had never had any children, so the thought of becoming a stepdad thrilled him. He had come from six generations of males only, so fathering four (mostly) adoring girls was like hitting the jackpot. He would be a dad the moment he became a husband, and he was more than ready for the role. Except for the distance with the oldest, it seemed that winning the girls' hearts would be a piece of cake. The stepparenting journey, however, can be deceptively simple before it starts.

Earl's wife had been left to raise all four girls on her own when her first husband had an affair and moved in with his girlfriend. She was managing a career, a household, the girls' activities, and five broken hearts, which caused her to sometimes "cave" on discipline and other battles she had no energy to fight. Her ex spent most of his time with his new family, visiting his girls only now and then, which created additional heartache. His absence caused the girls much fear, sadness, and self-doubt, which manifested itself in each girl differently as they grew up.

The second-oldest daughter had the roughest time, falling into a cycle of depression, self-abuse, and low self-esteem. At age thirteen, she began discovering boys but had no communication with her father to help her navigate the budding relationships. When her mom tried to guide and discipline her, the daughter would simply blame her for all her troubles and shut down.

Eventually, the daughter began turning from her mom to Earl, pouring out her heart during meltdowns, which had become a regular part of her life. Earl prayed for strength to listen, and he began to see his role as just being there to come alongside her and give an ear to her rants. He wasn't always able to hold his tongue, but he found that if she could just get out her fears and frustrations and feel heard, she would calm down and become civil again.

Earl's willingness to listen and be there for her acted like a balm to her troubled soul. He often ended their conversations by telling her that he loved her deeply, just as her mom and God did. They all saw what her decisions were doing to her heart and life, and they longed for her to make good choices, which Earl continually encouraged her to do.

Of all the girls, Earl's youngest stepdaughter had the closest relationship with him because he became the dad in her home when she was just three years old. When she turned fifteen, she made the choice to go live with her biological father, so a new chapter in Earl's stepparenting saga has begun. At the same time, the oldest daughter, who is now twenty-six and who has had nothing to do with him or his wife for almost ten years, has slowly started communicating and coming back into their lives.

After eight years of marriage, Earl now knows this up-and-down story is all part of the stepparenting journey. He's learned to pray his way through the bad and to wait for time and God to change things as the girls continue to evolve. He hovers in the good moments, locking them away in his mind and heart to feed off them in seasons of difficulty.

One such moment happened when his second stepdaughter called to talk one day. As she began talking about her problems with her mother, Earl felt a familiar defensiveness and was preparing to softly end the conversation when she suddenly said this:

> I know you have to go, and I appreciate your listening to me rant again…but I want to tell you, you are—and have been—just such a blessing to me and my family…to all us sisters and especially to Mom. You've been a dad when mine hasn't been there for us. We all love you so much and are so grateful for you, and we're so lucky to have you in our lives. You're the best thing that ever happened to our family.

Earl fell silent. Her fragrant words filled his heart, pushing all the painful nights into the background of his memory. After they hung up, he thanked God for these loving, life-affirming words. It's with this full heart that he faces the challenges of parenting four grown girls whose strained relationships with their biological dad continue. But Earl knows he's been called by God to stand in the gaps of the brokenness that preceded him and love his girls in whatever way they will allow. Thankfully, he knows he hasn't been called to do that alone.

RAYNA

It wasn't marital strife or a painful divorce that set off the chain of events that led Rayna to Danny. It was Danny's sudden singleness after the tragic death of his first wife. Left with a two-year-old and five-year-old, Danny spent the first year after her death feeling like life was swirling around him without him in it. Grace surprised him the day he met Rayna, causing his heart to suddenly wake up.

The first time Rayna saw him, her heart turned to Jell-O. He had come to lead worship at her church on Father's Day. As Danny softly shared his heartbreaking story, her sadness was laced with a twinge of guilt for the attraction she felt. A month later, fate brought them together backstage at an event, and when she got her own name wrong as they were introduced, she knew something disconcerting was happening. She pretended not to notice that she was counting how many times Danny happened by her booth during the hours she was working there just to say hi. A friend saw their obvious chemistry and took them to lunch so they could talk.

A week later, Danny dialed Rayna's number and asked her on his first date since the tragedy. Though his friends encouraged him to move forward, he couldn't help but feel strange at the newness happening inside his heart. They were like two schoolkids with a crush, but as dinner progressed, there was something more about her that was drawing him. He surprised even himself when he asked that night if she wanted to meet his kids, and he was relieved when Rayna did not flinch and simply said she did.

Danny's kids met Rayna and grew to love her during the months Rayna and Danny dated. They clearly had mama-hungry hearts, and they bubbled up with joy the night Danny and Rayna got engaged. When Danny's daughter turned to Rayna and said purposefully, "Mommy, would you like a glass of water?" Rayna's heart burst open, and she happily enveloped the new family God had brought to her life.

A few months later, her new daughter was twirling down the aisle as their flower girl, and with her baby brother toddling in with the ring, a new chapter of happiness for this sweet family seemed to be beginning. Rayna tried not to notice that a look of sadness intermittently surfaced on her precious stepdaughter's face as they continued celebrating into the night. It was a foreshadowing of the inevitable struggle that her daughter would face welcoming a new mom into her life.

When Rayna and Danny came home from their honeymoon, "WELCOME HOME, MOM AND DAD" was painted on a sign in the driveway. Danny's son had started to talk, and the first time he said "Mom," it was to Rayna, which solidified her joy. Their table was set for the life of happy endings...until Rayna discovered the next chapter in her story would hold some discomfort and difficulty. The reality of being a mom to two kids she hadn't birthed did not end up being quite as smooth as she initially thought. The first big challenge took place when her musician-husband took his first trip and she was left to parent on her own.

For Rayna to be the mom they needed, she would sometimes need to trade her kids' affection for their well-being. With Danny gone a couple of weekends each month, she had to learn to be strong enough to discipline them on her own. When she sent her daughter on her first of many time-outs, the little girl drew a picture of the family without her. Rayna's heart broke. Danny's first wife became "the nice mommy," and when the kids didn't like Rayna's discipline, they would cry for Mama Cyndi's return.

But in the midst of these small daggers to her heart, Rayna found that just when she felt like giving up, one of them would snuggle up and tell her she was their "favorite mommy." During the roller-coaster ride of her first year of parenthood, she learned not to let her stepchildren's up-and-down responses direct her love. She asked God daily to fill her with the perseverance of her call.

Rayna and Danny eventually gave birth to a daughter, and the moment she joined the family, she was beloved by all of them. Their child has now grown to become a teenager, and with her adult brother and sister, three children make up Danny and Rayna's pieced-together home.

Mama Cyndi continues to be an important part of their story. Shortly after she died, Danny's daughter asked him if he thought God ever let Mommy paint the sky. Those words inspired Danny to begin writing a book documenting Cyndi's life story. At the time, he didn't realize that his last chapter would introduce the second mommy God sent to him and his kids.

When *Mommy Paints the Sky* was published, Rayna's part in painting the family had already begun. Looking back, Rayna couldn't be more grateful that she was the one God chose to color their lives.

DIANA AND ED

Diana and Ed could never have imagined the love story that would rise from the ashes around them during the tense first days of their friendship. Truth be told, if they could, they would rewrite their story with a different start. Twenty years later, they see it as part of the reparative grace God has miraculously woven through their family. The path that brought them together was the devastation they have long put behind them—an affair between their spouses that tore their lives apart.

What began as a friendship of encouragement and comfort took a turn neither of them envisioned or anticipated. Perhaps the greatest irony was that the relationship between their spouses eventually ended, but their love grew over time to bring them a new start. Initially they leaned on each other for support and to provide some stability for their boys while their ex-spouses continued their up-and-down relationship. Attraction grew out of respect and admiration, but neither of them could possibly entertain the notion that there could be more there. After a year of trying to be open to new relationships by dating others, they eventually made peace with what God made clear to both of them. The only thing left to reconcile was that any kind of permanent relationship would inextricably tie them to the people responsible for breaking their hearts.

If Ed and Diana married, the exes who would co-parent their children would be the two people who destroyed their families. Though their exes were now with different partners, Ed and Diana would have to work with them in matters related to their children for the rest of their lives. The amount of grace this would cost their hearts seemed too great a price, and this is what initially kept them from pursuing a relationship. However, they could not deny what they saw in each other and the growing camaraderie between their boys, which had brought some steadiness to their lives. Ultimately the love that grew between them, and the family that had formed in front of them, led them from a five-year friendship to become husband and wife.

When Diana and Ed married and began co-parenting, their exes quickly became the "fun parents" while they brought stability through discipline. They supported each other with shared parenting goals, but it was hard to find a disciplinary rhythm with a custody schedule that regularly disrupted their lives. While Diana's boys were home, half the time Ed's son would be there too, and the changing dynamics brought many challenges. Add to that Ed's schedule as a fireman, and there were times when Diana was left to juggle the parenting all alone. Just when they would find their stride, one or two of the boys would be taken to their other family. When they returned, there was the inevitable "detox" to bring their behavior back to what they needed for their health and growth. The years of parenting brought so much upheaval, Ed and Diana barely had time for each other, let alone friends and family who could breathe life into them. But they hung on to each other and grew closer together as they learned to depend on God's presence and strength.

When Ed's son turned eighteen, he made the decision to come live with them. His years with Ed and Diana have given him a stability he draws from—not only in his soul but also in his relationship with his fiancée. He even went on to attend Bible college but ultimately decided to follow his father's career path. One of Diana's sons also followed in Ed's footsteps, and these two stepbrothers now have jobs as paramedics and firefighters as they start families of their own. Diana's other son continues to speak of the example Ed has been to him too— and recently made it a priority to come celebrate his stepdad at his retirement.

Diana's sons have come to embrace the gift Ed has been—not only to their mother but also in their values and direction. In the meantime, Ed's son affectionately calls Diana "Madre" because she was the mom who was partly responsible for changing the trajectory of his life. All three boys acknowledge that Ed and Diana's twenty-year marriage has brought them a permanence that has altered their stability. Now that two of the three boys are engaged, they know their future families will be impacted by Ed and Diana's love.

Diana and Ed tell very few people about the way their twenty-five year relationship started. It is a part of the story they don't often return to, yet they see God's amazing grace in transforming their loss into unexpected joy. They know their story showcases God's ability to put together fragments that seem irredeemable. For that reason, they graciously allowed me to include it in this book as an example of how God can work in broken lives.

DEBBIE

Debbie was certain she would never be divorced, so she never thought about what it would be like to blend a family. She had a great marriage, a great family, and a great life. She and her husband loved Jesus, served God with all their heart, and were devoted to living God's plan for them. But God's plan took a shocking turn when Debbie's husband told her that he had met another woman and was pursuing their relationship and that he wanted a divorce.

Debbie and her kids were left devastated, abandoned, and broken. Looking back, she doesn't know how she ever made it through those very dark days. God's mercy and grace kept Debbie together when her world fell apart.

She tried to embrace her new normal, though she had no experience being single, let alone parenting without a husband. Many months went by before she was finally able to settle into this unwanted chapter of her life. During this time, Debbie prayed for a lot of things, but meeting a man and getting remarried was not one of them. The man she met and eventually fell in love with, however, prayed every day for ten years to meet a godly woman with whom he could share his life. He believed God answered his prayer when he met Debbie.

Two years after they met, Debbie and Steve married, and the journey of blending their families with adult children began to take shape around them. Marrying Steve spurred Debbie to educate herself about becoming a stepmom, and it helped her realize her family was already blended before her marriage took place. Because of her husband's remarriage, others had already entered her children's narrative. This new awareness, along with everything she was learning for her own marriage, helped her become more intentional as their stepfamily began to form.

Looking back, Debbie knows if she had more understanding about the dynamics involved in stepfamilies, she may have done some things differently. She might have avoided some of the hurt they went through; however, she sees how the grace of God filled in their gaps. If she could advise anyone else marrying someone with adult children, she would tell them to let God set the pace and not try to speed up the process to become an instant family. She knows by experience that there is no substitute for time in allowing children the space to adjust to their dual-parent homes. Time has allowed Debbie's stepfamily to eventually make new memories, learn each other's personalities, walk through disappointments, and deal with conflict and resolution. Time has been Debbie's best friend in her stepparenting journey, and there is no substitute for what it has brought to her family's life.

Debbie also learned that she needed to give her husband space to have time alone with his kids, who were well into adulthood when Steve and Debbie married. She found that Steve's kids appreciated it when she gave them room to spend time with their dad. Her own kids needed time with her too, and Steve gave them space for that as they slowly accepted him into their family. Debbie's kids initially felt like Steve was a stranger in "their" house, and Steve gave them time and grace to acclimate to him even though it was now his and Debbie's home. By letting the kids set the pace, Steve and Debbie allowed them to be part of the process of creating this new chapter of blending their lives.

Steve's children were in their thirties when Steve and Debbie married, and Debbie knew they didn't need another mother. She felt her role was just to be their friend and an additional cheerleader in their lives. She knows their appreciation grows for her when they feel their dad is being loved well, cared for, and celebrated. That is the greatest gift she can give them, and she made her intentions clear at the wedding when she vowed to support them throughout their lives. Debbie wants to keep building her own unique relationship with them, and she is grateful for how that has happened and continues to grow.

Debbie and Steve's theme verse for their stepfamily is 1 Corinthians 13:8, which states simply, "Love never fails." Whenever they face difficulty, they go back to this verse and use it as their guide. With all the inevitable opportunities for conflict, hurt feelings, resentment, disappointment, and misunderstandings, Debbie and Steve have made 1 Corinthians 13 their family's blueprint. Their persistence to keep loving their kids has paid off, and after four years of marriage, Debbie believes their growing love will continue to see them through. The bond that holds their family may not be blood, but love and respect have woven them together. Debbie now looks back at her brokenness as the middle of her story because God used the gift of a stepfamily to bring a new ending of redemption to her life.

KRISTA AND DAVID

As they neared the last scene of the movie, Krista's husband turned to her and said, "Let's end this." After she got up to grab the remote, she suddenly realized it wasn't the movie he wanted to end. Everything went still, and Krista's heart shattered as he asked her for a divorce.

For weeks she tried patiently talking him out of it, knowing his last deployment along with his best friend's death had sent him reeling. PTSD had already left its mark on their young family, and Krista was used to managing the kids not only when her husband was gone but also much of the time he was home. But she never imagined in a million years that he would leave her—she and the kids had been the family that was always there for him. Nevertheless, his resolve made it clear there was no room for discussion; and they agreed that for the sake of the kids, she would move out with them to her parents' home. With a two-year-old daughter, a five-year-old son, and a new job to make ends meet, Krista began acclimating to her unchosen life.

After three years of single parenting, Krista met David, who was also divorced but had finished raising his children. His wife had left him for the soccer coach, so David had spent his kids' high school years living with the humiliation of a small-town affair that broke his family, his pride, and his heart. After his son and daughter graduated and moved on to college, David felt it was time to strike out to find a new chapter. Raising more kids was not necessarily on his wish list, but after he met Krista, it slowly became clear that she and her family were becoming much more to him than a checked box on an internet site. The more time he spent with Krista and her two kids, the more he felt called to permanently enter their lives.

Because their hearts were fragile, Krista and David moved slow. But as they progressed, Krista felt her parents' resistance. As much as they wanted Krista to be happy, they had grown used to parenting her children, so her relationship with David made them feel protective and attached. When David and Krista got engaged, Krista's mom was devastated. Though it wasn't the response she hoped for, Krista stood firm in her resolve to marry David because she knew he was a gift that God brought to her family's life. She could see it not only in the way he loved her but especially in the way he dedicated himself to her son and daughter. Watching David's commitment over the past five years of their marriage, Krista's mother has come to realize Krista was right.

Krista and David's first year of stepparenting was a roller coaster. Krista's son was mostly happy to have new older siblings, but Krista's daughter teetered between anger and despondency. Occasionally she would settle into acceptance, but her disrespectful attitude to Krista and David did little to mask her feelings. She did everything she could to hold David at bay, but because David and Krista had read up on the dynamics of stepfamilies, they both knew David's role would be important in his stepdaughter's life. David prayed for the strength to barrel through her indifference, and he reached out to God for the unconditional love he needed to keep filling the hole that had been left in her heart. He was called to tend what another man had broken apart.

Both Krista and David have found their inspiration from a simple wooden plaque that hangs on their living room wall. The words on it have become their daily prayer regardless of the state of their house. When Krista's daughter goes to bed and David says "I love you" from the hallway, he is often met with silence. From there, he walks to the living room and asks God to strengthen him with the words that have shaped his stepfather heart:

> I choose you,
> and I'll choose you over and over.
> Without a pause,
> without doubt,
> in a heartbeat,
> I'll keep choosing you
> Because God blessed me with you.

Krista also holds these words as her prayer as she embraces being a stepmom to David's adult children. Though her stepparenting looks very different than her husband's, she knows they will each face new and different challenges with the children they each had with their first spouse. For now, Krista has a front-row seat watching David love her growing children, and his willingness to persist in front of her daughter's barricaded heart reaches into her soul and deeply touches her. She thanks God for his unwavering commitment and prays the grace that has sustained him will uphold his heart as he continues to fight.

Because of their faith in the power of unconditional love, they know someday David's "I love you" will find its way into the saddened heart of his stepdaughter. And as an added sign of God's presence in their story, the name they pray for is the name her mama gave her, which happens to be Hope.

10

A Conversation with My Stepson

I am trusting that it is God's design that this book was published while my stepson is a teenager. Frankly, if I had given God my blueprint for this ending chapter, I might have preferred to interview Jordan when he was young and blissfully naive or when he was an adult reflecting back over his childhood. My boy is very much in process with his family journey, and like any other teenager, he is currently hot and cold with all his parents. We are far from the end of our story, but I asked him to reflect on his experience with me and stepfamily life.

This chapter was originally going to be called "Ten Things Your Stepchild Wishes You Knew," but Jordan perceptively realized that his story was unique and that he couldn't give a blueprint for all stepparents. So we decided to do this as an interview, and that way he could answer questions from his perspective about having a stepparent in his life. I have transcribed our conversation with as few edits as possible to maintain his voice.

LAURIE: What do you remember about the time when Dad and I were dating?

JORDAN: Losing my first tooth in your bathroom and you finding it the next day. Um, I remember my birthday…and your M&M's cake. And I remember one other time when there were helicopters and me and Dad were over at your house.

LAURIE: Do you remember there was a fire? Were you scared?

JORDAN: No. I don't remember being scared.

LAURIE: I'm glad. So let's move to our wedding. Do you remember any particular feelings? What was that experience like for you?

JORDAN: I was too young to really understand what was going on. I just thought it was like this giant party. So I was eating cake, having food, and dancing.

LAURIE: Did you know Dad and I were coming together?

JORDAN: Yes and no. I knew there was something going on—"Oh, they're getting married." But I didn't really know what it meant. I just thought you were going to be together more often I guess.

LAURIE: Do you remember the ring?

JORDAN: Of course. I remember I was the ring bearer, and I thought I was going to untie the ring from my pillow and hand you the ring. But that never happened. No one told me it was fake.

LAURIE: Aw, I'm sorry about that. Do you remember feeling happy at the wedding?

JORDAN: Yeah. There was cake, so yeah.

LAURIE: Do you remember what happened when we were leaving for our honeymoon?

JORDAN: Yeah, it was then when I realized something is going on. Why wasn't I going with my dad?

LAURIE: Do you remember the time period after we came back? That first year when your mom moved away?

JORDAN: I can't fully remember stuff till like fourth grade.

LAURIE: So let me take you back…

JORDAN: Well, I remember a couple spotty things. I remember sitting on the couch reading with you. I remember watching New Year's one year…And then you guys told me later it was 9:00.

LAURIE: Do you remember wanting me to come in and be with you before you went to sleep?

JORDAN: Oh, yeah. Of course.

LAURIE: Do you remember why you felt that way or wanted that?

JORDAN: Um, I know from a psychological view why I would want that…

LAURIE: Really? Why?

JORDAN: I was a child without a mother, so I grabbed whatever was there. You were there.

LAURIE: (laughing) Okay, but how did you feel with me?

JORDAN: I knew it wasn't completely normal. It was comforting. But it was more of a presence I needed.

LAURIE: Okay. Do you remember any other things you and I did together?

JORDAN: I remember a road trip we went on one time. I remember the play structure in the park.

LAURIE: Do you remember me volunteering in your classroom during elementary years?

JORDAN: Yeah.

LAURIE: As you look back, was it hard having two moms? Did you feel any conflict about balancing us both?

JORDAN: [Long silence] I think it wasn't difficult until later on. At first it was easy because life was simple. Once I got to sixth grade, it kind of started getting difficult because it was sort of like a conflict of interests, especially because you guys had a lot of rules that were different from the ones they had in Australia. Very different expectations. It was two completely different households.

LAURIE: Okay, I want to ask you about that later. But I was referring to the loyalty you might have felt to your mom. Did that affect your relationship with me?

JORDAN: Um, I mean…yeah, you were always kind of second to her because she was my mom. So that was always a thing. If she set a rule and you set a different rule, I would tend to follow hers.

LAURIE: Do you remember her asking you not to call me Mom?

JORDAN: Oh yeah.

LAURIE: How did you resolve that?

JORDAN: I don't know. I just didn't call you Mom when I was around her.

LAURIE: And that was fine? She was okay with that?

JORDAN: She didn't know. She just thought I stopped calling you Mom in general.

LAURIE: Does she still think that?

JORDAN: I don't know. I don't really care.

LAURIE: Has having two moms evolved to a different place now? Is it okay to love us both? Or is it still hard?

JORDAN: I think it's been that way for so long, it's not that hard. I'm used to it. For other kids to jump into having two moms, especially if they are my age, would be very, very difficult.

LAURIE: What are your best memories of our family times?

JORDAN: Thanksgivings. Those were some of my favorite times. Because we were with everybody. All the cousins.

LAURIE: Has it been fun having cousins through my side of the family?

JORDAN: Yeah, because I've never really had cousins. None of my extended family is blood related in a way. But we didn't really treat each other as cousins at first. Just friends. Then it slowly started to turn because of all the parties and holidays where we had to be together. We started hanging out more, and it felt more like family.

Laurie: Did you enjoy having family on my side of the family? Was that a plus?

Jordan: Oh yeah! That was definitely a plus.

Laurie: And what about friends?

Jordan: Definitely a plus too. Ian and Harry came from your friends. All those people came through you. I wouldn't have known them—or any of the friends I have. Those all came through you. And going to church at Oceanhills. Meeting all the people who are my friends now—most of them go to Oceanhills. Rob and all those people. I'd be in a very different place if it was not for those people.

Laurie: Really?

Jordan: Oh yeah. I'd be in a much worse place. I don't know where I'd be. The thing is, friends weren't really a thing for me growing up. Going through all those different schools, I hardly knew how to talk to people when I got to second grade. Especially not knowing how to read when everyone else knew how to read. The first day the teacher said, "Jordan, we're going to have someone show you around school." And Luke came up to me… it's funny, I remember exactly what he was wearing—a yellow Kobe Lakers shirt with the number 24 stitched on. White shoes. Red socks…he showed me all around the school, and then we went up to the hill where the play area was. And a group of us decided to play basketball. I had never touched a basketball in my life. And they were like, "We'll show you how to shoot. We'll show you how to play." I was so happy. I was thinking, "I don't know why you're talking to me, but I'm glad you are."

LAURIE: I remember volunteering in your second-grade class when I was paired up with Luke. I don't know if you remember that.

JORDAN: Yep, I do.

LAURIE: All the kids were reading so well, and you had only learned sight words in your other school.

JORDAN: Yeah.

LAURIE: I remember Mrs. Stokes said, "Don't worry. Just start reading with him after school, and he will pick it up." And by the end of the year, you were totally caught up.

JORDAN: I had a sixth-grade reading level at the end of second grade. That's one of the only things I still remember from second grade—that I left with a sixth-grade reading level. When I started, I didn't even know how to read.

LAURIE: Yeah, that's gigantic. So elementary school was good for you?

JORDAN: Some of the best years of my life.

LAURIE: Do you want to hear a secret?

JORDAN: I don't know.

LAURIE: Dad and I couldn't request a teacher, but if our child had a relational concern with another child in the same grade, we could request to have our child in a different class. And one time you said to us, "How come I'm never in class with Spencer?"

JORDAN: [Laughs]

Laurie: We did it because we felt like you already had so much on your own plate, and you and he were not good together. Can you understand why we did that?

Jordan: Oh, totally.

Laurie: We just felt like that would have been bad.

Jordan: Oh, it would have been. I probably would have started getting into fights. I remember getting into a fight with him at lunch because of a drop of milk on his sandwich. I still remember that—it was the first time I had to talk to the principal, and we both got a detention.

Laurie: I think you both eventually grew out of this stage. I know you guys have seen each other playing basketball over the years, and it's fine now. So…you mentioned before that going back and forth between our families was difficult. Did you do anything to prepare for the transition?

Jordan: Um…it was very different because of the situations and the people. It was like entering two completely different worlds. It was kind of like being in a country where the government was breaking down but the lower levels were doing okay. That's what it was like with my mom. But here, it was like the bottom area was breaking down and the government system was fine. Also, when all this happened, I didn't have my brother and sister, and I felt this void of loneliness. I had grown up with them, but they just sort of disappeared.

Laurie: But wasn't that because they were older? Didn't they leave before we lived together?

Jordan: Well, yeah, but…my sister just moved out. She just said she was moving out, and I really didn't know why.

LAURIE: After we got married, did you appreciate when we would go down and spend time with her?

JORDAN: Oh yeah, very much so. She and my brother had left, and suddenly I was the only one in the house. I was by myself, and it was like that nation crumbled and I was suddenly here alone with you guys. And I felt this emptiness.

LAURIE: So were you grateful for friends and family being in our life?

JORDAN: Oh, of course. That's why I loved hanging out with them. Being an only child, I didn't have anyone else to talk to.

LAURIE: So back to the transition. Stepparent experts describe it as having residence in two different countries, which was actually literal for you. But they say it's like that even when both families live in the same country.

JORDAN: That's totally accurate.

LAURIE: So, what were the biggest differences between your two families?

JORDAN: Um…the biggest difference was what I could spend my time doing. I was a lot more limited here on video games and stuff here. There, I could do more what I wanted. Fewer boundaries. And I could hang out with my stepsister there. But she was only there the first couple of years.

LAURIE: What other differences?

JORDAN: I mean…um, the food. That was different.

LAURIE: Would you say values were different?

JORDAN: Yeah. The values here were more Christian focused. Values there were more realistic.

LAURIE: What do you mean realistic?

JORDAN: Well…I mean, realism. The idea that "Life sucks, so these are values to help you get through life without it being horrible."

LAURIE: It doesn't sound very hopeful. Was it more a negative view?

JORDAN: Yeah, more negative and pessimistic…I've sort of become a combination of both. I'm not surprised when horrible things happen.

LAURIE: Do you see Christianity as being different from realism? Christianity acknowledges that bad things happen.

JORDAN: Christianity doesn't focus on that. They say the world is sinful and everyone is sinful, but they don't say you should expect stuff to go wrong. At church they don't say, "Everything is sinful, and everything is going to end up getting blown up. Get ready." That's what they said in Australia…especially when I was going into junior high and high school. They would tell me, "Okay, there are going to be a lot of people doing horrible things. Don't get stuck with them." They warned me so I would know when I see it.

LAURIE: Did you feel like we acknowledged that here?

JORDAN: Not really. Well, in a different way. They said it more like, "Yeah, bad things happen, and it sucks. Here is how you can get past that and deal with it." Here, it felt like you pitied me but…

LAURIE: You don't remember us coming to the junior high principal and dealing with what happened to you?

JORDAN: Yeah, but that felt different. It felt like "I'm sorry" was said too many times. In my other family, they just said "Yeah, it happens, but here's what you can do."

LAURIE: What did you hear here?

JORDAN: Here it was more like, "I'm so sorry, they should never have done that." I didn't feel empowered to fight back like I did there.

LAURIE: Hmm. Okay. So how did the differences play out in world-view values?

JORDAN: What they did wasn't that different because they both grew up in Christian homes…so they had that background.

LAURIE: Did you see the differences mostly in what was talked about?

JORDAN: Oh yeah. Very different.

LAURIE: What did they talk about that was different?

JORDAN: What they showed me—the movies and TV shows. I was exposed to more there. That's where my love for action movies came from. We had surround sound and watched action movies.

LAURIE: Sounds fun.

JORDAN: Also, what they talked about around the dinner table was very different.

LAURIE: How so?

JORDAN: Um, a lot of the dinner table was about cycling and stuff like that. They would talk a lot about what they were doing and the projects they were doing. What was going on. It was a much more analytical look at what was happening. Here, it was more of an emotional look at what was happening.

LAURIE: That's a great assessment.

JORDAN: This house was based on emotions...

LAURIE: (laughing) Maybe spiritual too?

JORDAN: Yeah. And theirs was based on analytical facts.

LAURIE: Was one more negative than the other?

JORDAN: Oh, yeah. Theirs was.

LAURIE: Like, critical?

JORDAN: Yes! Critical more than negative. Because they taught me people are stubborn. And when they mess up, they don't say they messed up. Everyone does that. In the workplace as well.

LAURIE: Let me ask you this—was it sort of like they looked more for the negative rather than the positive, and we looked more for the positive than the negative?

JORDAN: Yeah.

LAURIE: Is that the right way of assessing it? When they would talk about people, was it more like, "This is what they are doing wrong. This is what you should avoid," and we were like, "But look at the reasons behind it—give them the benefit of the doubt" kind of thing?

JORDAN: Yes. Very much so.

LAURIE: All right, here's another question. Anything you wish either family had done differently?

JORDAN: When are you referring to?

LAURIE: Just in general.

JORDAN: I wish I had been told more. About why my mom was leaving. I think that would have helped me understand stuff a little bit more.

LAURIE: Yeah.

JORDAN: Then I probably wouldn't have as much of a visceral reaction now to people leaving my life.

LAURIE: Do you understand why we didn't tell you more?

JORDAN: Um…I didn't think it was your place to talk about it because you weren't the one who was leaving.

LAURIE: We actually made a commitment to avoid saying anything to you that would move you away from her emotionally or in your mind. We wanted to support that relationship. That's what kept us from doing that.

JORDAN: Yeah, I understand. I think it's her conversation to have with me.

LAURIE: I think you're right. So, what about us? What could we have done differently? You mentioned preparing you more for the negative in the world…

JORDAN: Um, I think in general there was a lack of communication. Just everything. Even when you guys were getting married. I don't think I was told enough.

LAURIE: Really? Do you remember when we were dating, and you ran down the aisle at church and sat between us and put our arms around you?

JORDAN: Yeah.

LAURIE: So, there was a part of you that must have known we were coming together. You seemed happy.

JORDAN: Yeah, part of me knew. But part of me was also…from a psychological view, it was a motherly figure with my dad. The pieces fit.

LAURIE: So, there wasn't anything particular about me?

JORDAN: No.

LAURIE: Do you like me okay now?

JORDAN: [laughs]

LAURIE: Well, I love you.

JORDAN: [smirk edging toward a smile]

LAURIE: It feels like you're figuring out our relationship now. At first you just accepted me and didn't have too much trouble adjusting to me as a mom.

JORDAN: Well, it was because of how little I knew. I was just a kid. Ignorance is bliss.

LAURIE: Can you see anything good in it now—having someone in that place? Even though it wasn't the ideal person?

JORDAN: Mm-hm. I think it's a lot better than if I didn't.

LAURIE: Well, that's good.

JORDAN: So you're doing something right.

LAURIE: (laughs) Thanks. Okay, here's another question. Did you ever feel conflicted when the two sets of parents felt differently about something?

JORDAN: Um…I mean, I never really had to deal with that because the two situations were so different.

LAURIE: So you just told yourself, "Now I'm here…"

JORDAN: Yeah. "This is my mindset here. This is my mindset there." It was sort of like a switch. I would switch back and forth.

LAURIE: When did you do that?

JORDAN: The moment I got there. Sometimes it would take me a day or two.

LAURIE: Do you feel like we supported each other as families even though we were different?

JORDAN: Yeah, I guess. It's kind of difficult to see that as a kid.

LAURIE: Do you feel like either family talked about the other one? Or made it harder for you?

JORDAN: Yeah, a little. There wasn't a lot of talk. But every once in a while.

LAURIE: Do you remember us talking about them?

JORDAN: No. They would criticize you guys every once in a while.

LAURIE: Was that hard for you? Did you ever feel defensive?

JORDAN: No. I didn't take or push away the ideas they were putting out. I just let them sit on the table in a sense.

LAURIE: Hmm.

JORDAN: From a very young age I was observant and analytical. About everything.

LAURIE: Hmm.

JORDAN: Didn't matter which family. I was always watching. I would especially watch body language. I would know how people felt about what they were talking about. No matter who was talking. I would know how they felt by their body language.

LAURIE: But you didn't feel the need to defend either of your parents?

JORDAN: No, I just listened. Some were good points.

LAURIE: I imagine because we were Christians, it sometimes felt to them like we didn't know much or were limited in our perspective.

JORDAN: [silence]

LAURIE: Do you think it's different when kids meet their stepparents as little kids versus later in life?

Jordan: Yeah, it's very different.

Laurie: What's the difference?

Jordan: The difference with age is the knowledge they are given. For me, as a kid, I wasn't given a lot of knowledge or information, and I didn't need a lot then. If I was my age and it happened, it would be a very different conversation. There would be things I would need to know. And I think if your teenager is going through this, you have to tell them, prepare them, and give them information so they know what is going on.

Laurie: Would you say it's easier to bond when you are little?

Jordan: Very much easier. A kid will blindly look for a motherly or fatherly figure a lot easier than a teenager. Because of relationships in general—people are constantly falling out, so teenagers look at a relationship from a more distant point of view. You take a big step back and look at the person and say, "Do I want to have a relationship with them?" You think long and hard about it.

Laurie: Yeah.

Jordan: And you weigh all your options. Versus as a kid, you say, "Oh, cool, a new person in my life."

Laurie: Is there any kind of bonding that happens because of meeting your stepparent as a child? With all the traditions and time you spend together?

Jordan: There is a better surface-layer bond, but when they are teenagers, you can develop a deeper bond if they accept you. As a kid you are like, "I like this woman because she brings me cookies," but that would never work with teenagers.

LAURIE: That's true. But there was a lot that happened between the cookies and now.

JORDAN: Oh, of course.

LAURIE: Some of that must go somewhere. All the time and investment...

JORDAN: Of course. It goes to a place of "I trust them." So a kid will end up trusting you, but there is always the possibility that if you keep them in the dark about what happens, there could be a rift.

LAURIE: What do you mean "keep them in the dark"?

JORDAN: If I was never told anything and I was just told my mom and dad separated and now I have new parents and this whole different life...there would be an automatic rift when I got older and figured it out.

LAURIE: Oh, yeah. That would be weird. So what I hear from stepparents is the time factor makes a big difference in their relationship with their stepchild. There is more time invested if you come in when your child is young and are there as they grow older, but when a stepparent comes in when the child is a teenager, it's a shorter amount of time.

JORDAN: Yeah, I get that. But from a kid's point of view, it's part of that looking for a mother figure or father figure and what fits that square. When your child is older you have to gain their trust. It's not about giving them stuff that will make them like you, but it's about spending time with them and becoming a parent figure in a slow way. You have to be friends with them first to become their parent. You can't just suddenly be their parent and expect them to accept you.

LAURIE: Right. It's a relational authority over positional authority.

JORDAN: Exactly. You have to let them invite you in or else it's not going to work. Because if they don't invite you in, and you force your way in, they're never going to let you in.

LAURIE: Well, so let me ask you this. In the last year, I've been trying to let go more so you can become your own person. As a result, I haven't been spending as much time with you. Would you like me to be spending more time with you?

JORDAN: [Shrugs and shakes head no]

LAURIE: I've also felt like now is your time to bond with Dad. But I love you. Do you feel that?

JORDAN: Yeah.

LAURIE: I mean, you can't get rid of me.

JORDAN: [Silence]

LAURIE: Do you think that stepparents have a hard job?

JORDAN: Yes.

LAURIE: Why?

JORDAN: Because parenting is difficult. It doesn't matter if you are a parent or a stepparent. It's a difficult job.

LAURIE: Okay, so no difference between a parent or stepparent?

JORDAN: I think the problems you run into are different, but at the core of it, parenting is a difficult job.

LAURIE: When you say the problems you run into are different, what would be an example?

JORDAN: Like the relationship obstacles you have with a child. A child will always have a connection with his parents because they are his parents. It's a connection you will always have. With a stepparent, that connection has to be grown from somewhere. It doesn't appear out of nowhere.

LAURIE: Do you think being a stepparent is an important job?

JORDAN: Um…I mean, yeah. I think that's obvious. Of course being a stepparent is an important job. Being a parent is an important job. You are forming a child's life. If you don't take it seriously, and don't do it with passion, like 100 percent, you're not just failing yourself, you're failing the child.

LAURIE: Hmm.

JORDAN: And if you mess up bad enough, you're not just affecting yourself, but you're affecting the child. I think that goes for parents in general. What you are doing is becoming a role model for the child. And if you mess up hard enough, the child will see it, be impacted by it, and might even make the same mistakes later on in life.

LAURIE: Do you think there is grace if the parent says, "I made a mistake. I apologize."

JORDAN: It depends on the mistake. If it's just a disagreement or fight, then of course. But sometimes there are bigger ramifications to a mistake.

LAURIE: Like parents doing something long-term that is going to really affect the child?

JORDAN: Yeah. Or even something short-term that will affect the whole family. Like having a DUI accident. A child knowing that a parent was under the influence driving instills fear into a child. Knowing that the parent did that will scare the kid. Knowing that instills something into the brain—an immediate insecurity when you are around that person.

LAURIE: Like if you have an alcoholic parent and you watch the parent drink?

JORDAN: Yeah, it creates anxiety in a child. Same for when parents get in a big fight or get really angry and you don't know why—it creates a sense of anxiety. After a while, you expect it and learn to prepare for it, which some might think is good, but it's not.

LAURIE: That makes sense. Here's another question. Do you think that I had any influence on you growing up?

JORDAN: Of course.

LAURIE: What would be an example?

JORDAN: I mean there is nothing I can think of that was a sudden life-changing experience, but it was a lot of little things growing up. You can't really think of things your parents did that changed who you are because they formed who you are.

LAURIE: By their example?

JORDAN: By example, by what they tell you. Anything and everything you say to your child, it goes somewhere in their brain.

LAURIE: Would you say it would be different if they were telling you something and not living it?

Jordan: Depends on the child. Some would say, "I should probably listen to this even if they don't do it," and others would say, "They don't do it, so I don't care."

Laurie: Would you say that Dad and I lived what we taught? You can be honest.

Jordan: Yeah.

Laurie: When you think about the future, and your kids, and your relationship with Grammy, who is a stepparent, what do you think about grandparents who are stepparents?

Jordan: I don't think of them as stepparents. They are just grandparents.

Laurie: Almost like they are grafted in?

Jordan: Yeah. There is no such thing as a step-grandparent. Grandparents treat their step-grandchildren the same.

Laurie: As you look back on your life, do you think God might have been using me to fill in some gaps in your life?

Jordan: Um, I mean…obviously, yeah. The lack of having an immediate mother. That's obvious.

Laurie: Do you see how God blessed me the same way?

Jordan: I don't think this is a blessing. [laughs]

Laurie: You're wrong. Can you think of why being in your life was a blessing for me?

Jordan: Not having to go through pregnancy and having a child?

LAURIE: [laughs] Okay, that may be true, but God blessed me. And in an indirect way, your mom blessed me because I was able to step in and help raise you. Okay, so, any last words to stepparents? I know you are still in the middle of figuring things out right now.

JORDAN: Recognize that you technically aren't the parent because you aren't their biological parent, and don't try to replace that parent if you are stepping into that position—unless the child invites you into that position. But also, don't be afraid to be a substitute for that position. If you are going to be a parent, be a parent. Just don't pretend the other parent doesn't exist. That's something that some of my friends have run into—some stepparents just come in and act like they are the best parent, and they are trying to one-up the parent who left. And you are no longer growing the child at that point, you are growing your own ego. You have to respect the biological parent relationship. Because regardless of what the biological parent does, a lot of times the child will still go back to that parent if they have a chance. In some ways, as a stepparent, you are at the same level, but you aren't. Because you don't have blood relationship. You are second in the relationship status.

LAURIE: The stepparent is related to you by choice. The biological parent is in you. But does the amount of time you've spent together make a difference?

JORDAN: Yes, but I think it's the effort you put into the time. Not the amount of time. It's the parenting love you put into them.

LAURIE: Okay. Thanks so much for doing this. And I just want to say I love you. Again.

JORDAN: [Getting up and walking away. Quietly, mumbling under his breath] Love you too.

Jordan, if you read this interview as an adult someday, I want to deeply thank you for doing it. Your words were very insightful, and I think they made the perfect end to this book. However you end up remembering our relationship, I hope you know that I'll always be crazy about you. And I'll always be grateful that I was the one God brought to your pool.

I'll never regret jumping in.

Notes

CHAPTER 1: WELCOME TO THE POOL

1. Amelia Watkins, "A Step-Child's Guide to Step-Parenting," *Great Kids, Great Parents* (blog), *Psychology Today*, November 30, 2016, https://www.psychologytoday.com/us/blog /great-kids-great-parents/201611/step-childs-guide-step-parenting.

2. Lindsey Phillips, "Stepping Up to the Challenge," *Counseling Today*, May 29, 2019, https:// ct.counseling.org/2019/05/stepping-up-to-the-challenge/.

3. Anna de Acosta, "11 Stepmom Facts: Research from negative outcomes to positive solutions," (blog post), July 11, 2017, https://www.annadeacosta.com/blog/-11-stepmom-facts.

4. C.S. Lewis, *The Four Loves* (San Diego, CA: Harcourt Brace, 1991), 121. Originally published in 1960.

5. Wevorce, "Multiple Divorces Strain Kids," January 9, 2017, https://www.wevorce.com/blog /multiple-divorces-strain-kids/.

6. "In reality, [stepparents] have very little control—especially in the beginning." Diana Weiss-Wisdom, "7 Key Components for Successful Stepparenting," *Divorce*, April 11, 2016, https://www .divorcemag.com/articles/7-key-components-for-successful-stepparenting.

CHAPTER 2: PARTY OF TWO—
PLUS ONE (OR TWO OR THREE...)

1. Wednesday Martin, *Stepmonster: A New Look at Why Real Stepmothers Think, Feel, and Act the Way We Do* (Boston, MA: Houghton Mifflin Harcourt, 2009), 93.

2. Ron Deal, *The Smart Stepfamily: Seven Steps to a Healthy Family* (Bloomington, MA: Bethany House, 2014), 101.

3. James Bray and John Kelly, *Stepfamilies: Love, Marriage and Parenting in the First Decade* (New York, NY: Broadway Books, 1999), 24.

4. Bray and Kelly, 11.

5. Bray and Kelly, 12.

CHAPTER 3: MAKING ROOM

1. Martin, 131.

2. Alexia Fernandez, "Gwyneth Paltrow Says Backlash to 'Conscious Uncoupling' from Ex Chris Martin Was Brutal," *People*, March 18, 2019, https://people.com/movies/gwyneth-paltrow -backlash-conscious-uncoupling-was-brutal/.

3. Martin, 153.

4. Deal, 137.

5. Bray and Kelly, 83.

CHAPTER 4: THE WEIGHT OF INFLUENCE

1. Kendra Cherry, "The Age Old Debate of Nature vs. Nurture," Verywell Mind, June 3, 2020. https://www.verywellmind.com/what-is-nature-versus-nurture-2795392.

2. Bray and Kelly, 57-58.

CHAPTER 5: THE INSIDE JOB OF STEPPARENTING

1. Deal, 113.

2. Deal, 115-118.

3. Martin, 87.

4. Cited in "Common and Unrealistic Expectations About Stepfamilies," FamilyEducation, https:// www.familyeducation.com/life/stepfamilies/common-unrealistic-expectations-about-step families.

5. Cited in Elizabeth Church, "The Poisoned Apple: Stepmothers' Experience of Envy and Jealousy," *Journal of Feminist Family Therapy* 11, no. 3 (2000): 3, https://doi.org/10.1300/J086v11n03_01.

6. Church, 3.

7. Church, 4.

8. Martin, 90.

CHAPTER 6: WHEN UNFAIR IS OKAY

1. Lewis Smedes, *Forgive and Forget* (New York, NY: Harper & Row Publishers, 1987), xvi.

2. Smedes, 113.

3. Phillip Yancey, *What's So Amazing About Grace?* (Grand Rapids, MI: Zondervan, 2002), 79.

4. Smedes, 133.

5. Smedes, 131.

CHAPTER 7: FINDING PERSPECTIVE

1. Martin, 89-90.

2. Walter Wangerin, *Ragman: And Other Cries of Faith* (New York, NY: HarperOne, 2004).

CHAPTER 8: ADVICE FROM THE TRENCHES

1. "What is 'hitting the wall' during a marathon and how can you avoid it? *Runners World*, February 4, 2019, https://www.runnersworld.com/uk/training/marathon/a774858/how-to-avoid-the-wall-and-cope-if-you-hit-it/.

2. Cited in Valerie Strauss, "Best commencement speeches never given," in *Answer Sheet*, a blog from the *Washington Post*, May 19, 2012, https://www.washingtonpost.com/blogs/answer-sheet/post/best-commencement-speeches-never-given/2012/05/18/gIQAvaRQZU_blog.html.

About the Author

Laurie Polich Short is a speaker, author, preacher, and stepmom. A graduate of Fuller Theological Seminary, Laurie has served on the staff of four churches over the past thirty years. She is currently a member of the teaching team at Oceanhills Covenant Church in Santa Barbara.

Laurie has spoken to more than 500,000 people at conferences, colleges, and churches around the country, and her popular teaching videos on RightNow Media have been viewed by more than 250,000 people all over the world. Her three most recent books are *40 Verses to Ignite Your Faith: Surprising Insights on Unexpected Passages* (April 2019), *When Changing Nothing Changes Everything* (May 2017), and *Finding Faith in the Dark* (August 2014). She has also written fourteen books for youth and youth workers.

Laurie has been featured on PBS and Focus on the Family, and in 2018 she cofounded SheGrowsConference to promote mentoring among women. She lives in Santa Barbara with her husband, Jere, and stepson, Jordan.

Follow Laurie on YouTube, Instagram, and Facebook

@lauriepshort

Find speaking clips and more information about her ministry at

www.laurieshort.com

KARYN PURVIS, PhD
& LISA QUALLS with Emmelie Pickett

from the author of *The Connected Child*

The
Connected
Parent

Real-Life Strategies for Building Trust and Attachment

THERE IS HOPE FOR EVERY CHILD, EVERY PARENT, AND EVERY FAMILY

Parenting under the best of circumstances can be difficult. And raising children who have come to your home from "hard places," who have their own set of unique needs, brings even more challenges. You may have discovered that the techniques that worked with your birth children are not working with your adopted or foster child. Renowned child-development expert Dr. Karyn Purvis gives you practical advice and powerful tools you can use to encourage secure attachment in your family. You will benefit from Karyn's decades of clinical research and real-world experience. Coauthor Lisa Qualls demonstrates how you can successfully implement these strategies in your home, just as she did in hers. You will learn how to simplify your approach using scripts, nurture your child, combat chronic fear, teach respect, and develop other valuable tools to facilitate a healing connection with your child. *The Connected Parent* will help you lovingly guide your children and bring renewed hope and restoration to your family.

To learn more about Harvest House books and
to read sample chapters, visit our website:

www.harvesthousepublishers.com

HARVEST HOUSE PUBLISHERS
EUGENE, OREGON